The Reality of Schizophrenia

Previously a psychiatric social worker for fourteen years, Gwen Howe now manages a Health Authority day centre and support service for schizophrenia sufferers and their families. She is a member of the Council of Management of the National Schizophrenia Fellowship and is also one of its professional advisers. She frequently gives talks on schizophrenia and is currently involved in training voluntary counsellors for work with this illness.

Gwen Howe has written another book, *Schizophrenia: A Fresh Approach* (David and Charles), which has recently been revised and reprinted. She has two grown-up daughters and lives with her college lecturer husband in Essex.

Some other Faber health titles

THE FABER BOOK OF MADNESS
Roy Porter

THE HEALTH CARE CONSUMER GUIDE
Robert Gann

THE EPILEPSY REFERENCE BOOK
Jolyon Oxley and Jay Smith

CHILDREN WITH SPECIAL NEEDS
Richard Woolfson

EXAMINING DOCTORS
Donald Gould

KEEPING WELL: A GUIDE TO HEALTH IN RETIREMENT
Anne Roberts

THE MENOPAUSE
Mary Anderson

THE FERTILITY AND CONTRACEPTION BOOK
Julia Mosse and Josephine Heaton

ALZHEIMER'S DISEASE: THE LONG BEREAVEMENT
Elizabeth Forsythe

MULTIPLE SCLEROSIS: EXPLORING SICKNESS AND HEALTH
Elizabeth Forsythe

DRUG USE AND ABUSE
James Willis

EVERYWOMAN: A GYNAECOLOGICAL GUIDE FOR LIFE
Fifth Edition *Derek Llewellyn-Jones*

ANOREXIA NERVOSA: THE BROKEN CIRCLE
Ann Erichsen

AGORAPHOBIA
Ruth Hurst Voce

The Reality of Schizophrenia

GWEN HOWE

faber and faber

LONDON · BOSTON

First published in 1991
by Faber and Faber Limited
3 Queen Square London WC1N 3AU

Photoset by Wilmaset, Birkenhead, Wirral
Printed in Great Britain by Clays Ltd, St Ives plc

© Gwen Howe, 1991

Gwen Howe is hereby identified as author
of this work in accordance with Section 77
of the Copyright, Designs and Patents Act 1988.

A CIP record for this book is available from the British Library.

ISBN 0 571 16285 1

For all those who cannot tolerate unnecessary suffering

Contents

Acknowledgments

My gratitude to the many brave, determined people, affected as sufferers or their relatives by this illness, who have shared with me over the years their pain, their frustration and, occasionally, their triumphs. This book is about them.

I would like to thank Susanne McDadd for her faith in my work and for eventually, after several external crises, bringing it to the notice of her colleague at Faber and Faber, Roger Osborne, who has proved so rewarding to work with. Similarly, I am grateful to my agent and friend, Vanessa Holt, for her enthusiasm and constructive help at all times.

I am indebted to my colleague Dr Bernard Heine for the time he has given to reading the proofs and for his constructive criticisms. My thanks also to Audrey Eldrige, Tina Kent, Valerie Robinson and my daughters, Chris and Sal, for their patient reading of parts of the draft manuscript and for their helpful comments. Once again, I would like to record my appreciation of the superb service provided by hospital librarian Maureen Rouse.

Finally, a special tribute to my husband Derek for his constant support, patience and good humour.

Introduction

Schizophrenia is a common condition. It attacks one person in every 100 in all types of society and culture the whole world over. Yet it remains shrouded in secrecy, ignorance and fear. I have come to believe that this denial in all of us is responsible for more misery and pain and wasted lives than the illness itself. Most cases of schizophrenia occur in young people in the prime of life, between the ages of sixteen and twenty-five. Too many of them experience agonizingly long delays before a diagnosis and urgently needed treatment are provided. Later, they can remain in ignorance of what has happened to them and of *how to protect themselves in the future*. Those who are fortunate enough to fight their way back to reasonable health may then find that the word 'schizophrenia' militates against them at every turn.

This book is an attempt to do something about this tragic toll of human suffering and wastage. It starts by demonstrating what so often happens to families seeking help for a son or daughter who is developing the illness and what it may feel like for the young person. It goes on to look into the background of the attitudes that influence the current approach to schizophrenia and highlights the failings and avoidable misery inherent in such an approach by describing the experiences of some of the brave people I have known during the years I have worked with this illness. Finally, I recommend another way forward; *a preventive approach* to minimize all the suffering and waste that occurs at the present time.

As the point of writing this book is to reveal the truth that is crippling many thousands of sufferers and their families, there is a danger that I might seem to dismiss all too lightly the dedicated work of some of the colleagues I have been privileged to meet and work with. This book is not about them and others like them, nor about their patients and clients, some of whom survive to enjoy life after schizophrenia. It is about the rest and it is about a system that is surely more insane than any mental illness.

Finally, my apologies to anyone who has experienced schizophrenia who is irritated by my constant use of the word 'sufferer'. Until we have a better word, I cannot come to terms with describing people as, say, 'coeliacs', 'diabetics' or 'schizophrenics', and prefer to use the word sufferer when discussing someone's particular disorder.

Gwen Howe
November 1990

1 · Steven

It is 1985 and Steven is planning to go to college to study engineering. An intelligent sixteen-year-old, he is popular with his peers and has had the same small group of close friends since his junior school-days. Team sports and a busy social life take up most of his spare time, but he seems to be coping well with his studies. He has an easy relationship with his parents and gets on reasonably well most of the time with his younger brother. On the whole, life is good for Steven but he has little time for such considerations!

Towards the end of his first term in the sixth form, Steven's mother starts to feel a little anxious about her elder son. He has given up some of his sporting activities over the past weeks and also seems to be going out less than usual with his friends. At first she wonders if he has fallen in love with a girl who has more claims on his time than his old interests, but nothing happens to suggest this is the case. She would be hard put to explain why, but his mother feels that something is wrong; there is a change in her son that she does not understand and cannot quite explain, even to herself. Although it would be understandable if Steven's schoolwork were taking up more of his time, she suspects that he is not doing any extra studying, or doing anything in fact, with the extra time he has on his hands.

During the following weeks, Steven spends more and more time in the home and yet is unusually distant and unapproachable. He seems to be spending a lot of his time in his room, playing jazz records very loudly and seemingly doing nothing but lying and staring into space. When she talks about this with family and close friends, Steven's mother immediately receives reassurances that this is all part of growing up; he's probably in love or something, or needing to 'find himself' or whatever!

Before very long, her husband starts to share some of his wife's anxiety about their elder son, who has now given up the rest of his sporting activities, with no signs of taking up other interests to replace these. More worryingly, when his friends call he will not even go to the door to talk to them. Steven seems to be unhappy and remote, but his father's attempts to reach out to him are quickly rebuffed. When he decides to mention his concern on a routine visit to his GP, the doctor responds in much the same way as family and friends before him; not to worry, it's all part of growing up! Later, at a school Open Evening, the staff proclaim Steven to be a star pupil and a joy to teach. Only the PE teacher grumbles that the boy has let him down badly by acting out of character and backing out of two school teams.

At the end of the school year Steven does well in his exams, and his parents are still trying to convince themselves that the changes they have seen in him are just part of his growing up. This is not too easy when they are aware that even Steven's oldest friends have given up calling, their persistent efforts to involve him in their activities thwarted by his increasingly rejecting manner. As time goes on, his mother finds that Steven seems to be avoiding everyone except for herself. Whenever she is alone in the house, he seems to seek out her company while remaining remote and distant. She is becoming unhappily aware of his deep misery, but her attempts to find out what is wrong merely provoke irritable outbursts and accusations that she fusses too much. When anyone else joins them, Steven promptly disappears, and tends to snap at his father and younger brother if they attempt to talk with him. Most of his time is spent alone in his room, seemingly doing nothing but listening to the same few noisy jazz records. He is clearly having trouble sleeping and seems to be up most of the night, making endless cups of tea and stodgy snacks. Perhaps not surprisingly, his mother finds it more and more difficult to waken him in the morning. Tentatively, she brings up the subject once more with their GP, who privately wonders what is the matter with these parents who seem determined to fret about their healthy, attractive son. He points out that it is not surprising that the boy is awake half the night if he has given up all his energetic activities, probably resting in his room all evening anyway. As for his insatiable appetite, that's what she should expect from a young man of his age. Perhaps she worries too much and things will be a lot better when Steven has to stand on his own two feet away at college? Feeling foolish, but not really reassured, the mother walks slowly home and discusses the doctor's comments with her husband. Sadly they express amazement that they seem to be watching their son turn into a stranger while everyone around them is oblivious to this and to their concern.

As it happens, the doctor remembers this visit a few months later when Steven comes into his surgery several times in as many weeks with trivial ailments that seem to be of a hypochondriacal nature. This is certainly not characteristic of this previously healthy boy and he decides that it might be worth referring him for a psychiatric out-patient appointment, particularly as he is due to go away to college in the autumn. The doctor is not surprised, however, when this referral results in the psychiatrist writing to him to say that there seems to be nothing at all wrong with Steven, except that he is fed up with his mother fussing over him. The letter goes on to explain that the mother has been advised that it is normal for a boy of Steven's age to spend long hours alone in his room listening to records, and that they should understand his need to choose to give up old activities if that is what he wants, etc., etc. Perhaps they should learn to give him more 'space' and stop fussing over him? Anyway, going away to college will probably be the making of this over-protected boy.

After this, the parents again feel bewildered and humiliated. It seems that even the experts are determined that there is nothing wrong with Steven; if they are right, what is it that has changed his personality so drastically, and why is he so unhappy? Unfortunately Steven is now very angry with his parents and with the GP for arranging this referral to a psychiatrist. Even if they knew where else to seek help, his parents would be very wary about doing so after such negative experiences and increasing objections from their previously easygoing son.

DISCUSSION

Let us pause and consider; what has been happening up to now to this unhappy teenager? Over the past twenty months, the parents have seen a dramatic personality change, *for which there is no satisfactory explanation*. There were early stages of withdrawal followed more recently by quite definite avoidance behaviour. Steven's eating habits and sleeping pattern have changed, so that he is more active during the night than in the daytime, when he now spends most of his spare time lying on his bed. Previously athletic and sociable, he now has little energy and seeks out only his mother's company, while remaining remote and becoming irrationally critical of her. He is irritable and loses his temper quickly, without any apparent provocation. Finally, Steven is clearly desperately unhappy.

There are ample signs here that Steven is sick and needing help; signs that merit serious investigation rather than avoidance and which may reasonably lead to the suspicion of the presence of a common cluster of symptoms we presently call schizophrenia. If Steven is developing such an illness, then we may expect a steady deterioration when he leaves home. This will probably go unnoticed for a while in his new surroundings at college, amongst strangers. His peers will pronounce him 'a loner', lecturers may see little of him, and nothing is likely to happen until a breakdown is imminent and his behaviour becomes overtly embarrassing or a real cause for concern. The time-lag may well be a year or two, but probably the stress of being away from home when he is so vulnerable will speed things up. Meanwhile, this previously care-free, talented boy will be going through a lonely nightmare in which his studies will almost certainly fall by the wayside. His parents will have their suspicions about this, but feel helpless to intervene, particularly as he insists everything is 'OK, thank you!' By the time his illness can no longer be ignored, Steven will be unrecognizable as the boy who started to give up his hobbies and his friends so long ago, but the change will have been so gradual that for some considerable time *only those closest to him could see it*.

BREAKDOWN!

And so, as might be expected, the next cry for help comes from outside the family because Steven's behaviour is no longer just strange *for him*, but strange by any standards. His landlady becomes very concerned and she contacts the college for help. A doctor examines Steven and suggests that he should go into hospital for a few days, so that they can find the best way to help him. Steven refuses to consider this, so the doctor settles for prescribing medication for him, insisting that he should take this and see him again in a week's time. The following weekend the police find Steven crouching, shivering and incoherent, in the corner of a deserted car-park late at night. They take him up to the local psychiatric hospital for assessment, where he is eventually admitted to an acute ward. The patient is confused and incoherent a lot of the time, and at other times he is expressing ideas of being hunted by secret agents who know him to be a spy. He believes his parents and the hospital staff to be part of a conspiracy to extradite him to some obscure country waiting to bring him to justice. Not surprisingly, Steven is terrified and distrusting of all initial efforts to calm him.

His parents respond to the news of their son's admission to hospital with mixed feelings. A social worker has explained to them that Steven is detained under Section 2 of the Mental Health Act 1983, which allows for assessment and appropriate treatment in hospital for up to twenty-eight days (for a more detailed discussion on the mental health law, see Chapter 6). Sick at heart that their long-held fears have been confirmed, they are nevertheless relieved that now something will have to be done to help their son. However, if they expect to learn more about what has been happening to Steven, they are soon disappointed. Although the hospital doctors have no real doubts about the diagnosis, they do not confide in the parents when they rush to visit their son. Instead, they are told that Steven has had some sort of adolescent disturbance, *probably due to the stress of living away from home* and not being able to cope with his course work; perhaps they have been too ambitious for him careerwise, encouraging him to take on studies beyond his natural ability? It seems that Steven has been put on some sort of medication. Although neither he nor his parents are given any real explanation about its function, the possibility of early side-effects is mentioned, and they are told that one overwhelming advantage of Steven being in hospital is that it gives the doctors a chance to monitor his response to the drug. It seems, they learn, that he should continue to have this medication for 'a little while', anyway.

During the next few weeks, the worst aspects of the schizo-phrenic nightmare fade away. Steven is to be discharged home to his family, to continue the process of getting over his 'breakdown' and to consider carefully whether he should eventually resume his studies. The psychiatrist is not in favour of him returning to college and recommends instead that he should attend a day centre in his home town for a while. No one has discussed with Steven the experiences he has had nor the events that led to his admission to hospital. Although he is no longer scared that something awful is going to happen to him, and sometimes he feels happier than he has for several years, Steven has no idea he has been ill; he feels he has been conned into having medication when he does not need it and that the long nightmare he has been living through will end only when he gets out of hospital. He has no intention of prolonging it by having more 'treatment', so he adamantly refuses to discuss attending a day centre, and the subject is dropped.

As for the family, younger brother Gary hopes things are going to change now, but he is singularly unhappy at the thought of Steven coming home as he has become a little afraid of his brother recently and very embarrassed about his strange manner if anyone visits the house. Their parents, on the other hand, are elated that Steven is at last getting some help. They have already seen dramatic improvements in their son, who is talking to them again and seems glad to see them when they visit. He is sleeping better, his young face has lost some of its haggard, tortured appearance and most of his tenseness has gone. He is less remote and no longer flies into inexplicable rages. However, his parents often find him lying on his bed when they visit the hospital and he seems to have no energy or motivation to do anything at all. This is the one aspect of Steven's illness that his father has managed to discuss with the hospital staff, and has been told that they must be patient; the lethargy will pass with time. Before they take him home, the nurse in charge tells them that Steven has been referred to a psychiatrist in their home town and that his GP will be asked to arrange for Steven to be given his medication in the form of a fortnightly injection for the time being. This is important, it seems, and the next one is due in ten days' time.

HOMECOMING

Once home, Steven seems rather frail and lost. Whereas the daily routine of the hospital involved him in a certain amount of activity, albeit modest, such as helping to lay the table, taking his turn at washing up, making a trip to the hospital shop, and spending a couple of hours at Occupational Therapy, he now shows no incentive to exert himself even this far. His parents, having been told to be patient, do not like to force the issue. Steven lies either on his bed or on the settee downstairs and seemingly 'vegetates', as he never picks up a book or newspaper, and shows no interest in watching television either. His parents feel this inactivity cannot be good for him, and their fears seem to be confirmed as he becomes rather more lifeless with each new day. They seek advice from the GP, who tells them that the local psychiatrist will be assessing Steven's progress at his out-patients' clinic. He mentions that the hospital's discharge letter recommends that Steven should attend a day centre, and this would help keep him occupied, wouldn't it? Relieved, his parents tentatively take up this point with Steven, but he tells them he is not wasting his time attending a day centre; he must get back to college before he really falls too far behind. Instinctively, his parents realize this is not the time for Steven to go away again, let alone to resume his studies, but they have to admit that he comes to life only when he talks about college. They drop the subject of the day centre, and Steven continues to sit around doing nothing until one day he tells his mother that the medication makes him feel sleepy and, as he wants to get back to college, he will need to come off it. This time, his mother says he really must discuss this with the new doctor when he sees him, as she is sure he should not come off the medication so soon. After spending over an hour getting Steven out of bed next morning for his out-patients appointment, she accompanies him, taking with her a note of several matters that she and her husband are concerned about. However, the psychiatrist asks the young man if he wants his mother to join them in the interview and, when Steven says he thinks not, she finds herself politely waved out of the room. She is not given the chance to go back in to see the psychiatrist later. On their way home, her son tells her that the doctor is very pleased with him but agrees that Steven is really 'slowed down', so the dosage of his medication is to be halved . . .

It is not long before the parents notice a change in Steven, perhaps nearly as dramatic as when he was in hospital. He is more lively, alert and intent on pursuing his plans for returning to college, but he is jumpy and edgy with the family and is starting to walk the house again at night. Although he is so keen to take up his studies once more, he shows absolutely no sign of attempting to read a magazine, or even a news headline, let alone opening his college books. The parents are by now feeling anxious again a lot of the time; his mother finds that Steven seems to be relating only to her, as before, and she feels that things are not very different now from those awful days a couple of years ago before Steven went to college. Not knowing where to turn next, she pays a visit to the GP with her new worries about her son. The doctor points out that the psychiatric services are responsible for Steven's mental health at present but that recovery from a nervous breakdown is usually slow; she really must not expect too much too soon. Moreover, the fact that his medication has been cut down does not seem to suggest that the psychiatrist is disappointed in Steven's progress, does it?

Once again, a seemingly reasonable answer has been provided for parents who nevertheless sense that all is not as it should be. Unhappily, they still know nothing about their son's illness; at one point a 'psychotic episode' was mentioned at the hospital, with no further information when Steven's father repeated the phrase questioningly. In any event, they gather he has had a nervous breakdown, from which people apparently recover! They were told that it was important for Steven to continue with his medication 'for a while'. However, he insists that this is what makes him drowsy, and now the new doctor has reduced it already, so perhaps Steven is right and the medication does not suit him? And it is so nice to see him get back some of his old energy! But why does he seem angry again, tending to snap at his father and brother for no reason, and why can't he sleep at night, even going off for midnight walks on his own?

A few months pass, with little or no change, except that the members of the household find it increasingly difficult to relax in their own home. Far from recovering from his breakdown, as his parents had confidently believed he would, Steven sits and broods most of the day if his mother makes him get out of bed; otherwise he stays there until the early evening. When he eventually comes downstairs, having made no effort to wash or tidy himself up, he makes a bee-line for the fridge and larder and helps himself to frequent snacks of sweet, stodgy food, accompanied by countless cups of tea. He is hostile to his father and brother and very possessive about his mother, who nevertheless finds him remote and almost like a stranger.

In the early days of Steven's illness, his parents used to turn to family or friends with their fears; although they could not come up with solutions, their moral support was welcome. However, the stigma of mental illness in our society tends to turn families 'in on themselves'. This can be because of feelings of embarrassment and shame or because of a loyalty and protectiveness to the sick person and the need to cover up unpredictable or strange behaviour. In turn, relatives and friends may be reluctant to get involved and tend to prefer to persuade themselves that all is well really. Steven's parents are having the same experience as others before them, and just when they most need support, find themselves feeling alone and alienated in a familiar community. There seems to be no one with whom they can share the burden of their problems and fears.

Their various attempts to see Steven's new psychiatrist have been frustrated by messages that he will be pleased to see them *with Steven*, but not on their own as he considers this would be unethical. Bewildered by this response, they can only imagine he does not understand what is happening in their home. How on earth can they talk in front of their son about their fears for his future and their frustrations with him? In any event, they have had plenty of experience recently of his reaction to any comment or suggestion they put to him. He is so much on the defensive that everything is taken as a criticism, and he has told them he knows just what is being said about him behind his back, too, which mystifies them further.

This depressing phase is brought abruptly to a close when Steven returns from his next two-monthly out-patients' clinic appointment. The doctor has agreed he may benefit from living away from home and, in view of Steven's consistent desire to take up his studies again, he has backed his application to return to his old college. His mother is shocked by this news; she asks her son if the doctor realizes that he has no energy during the day, has great difficulty getting up before evening-time and has not even opened any of his college books since he came home. Steven flies into a rage at this and tells her the doctor understands he needs 'some space' and some peace from her constant nagging and criticisms. The doctor further reckons that if Steven has had the incentive to write to the college and to make arrangements about receiving another grant for his studies, then he deserves to have a try. What he needs is a challenge and something to get up for each day. His mother is puzzled by most of this, but she can see some logic in her son's last statement. She tells herself that she does not have the knowledge or expertise of the doctor, who surely must know what is best for the boy. Nevertheless, she is frightened for Steven.

RETURN TO COLLEGE

It is with relief that Steven's parents learn that he has been referred to the GP practice which serves the college, so that he can have his regular injection; the hospital doctor feels he should continue with this for a while as there are sure to be extra pressures when he resumes his studies.

It is noticeable that Steven comes home very soon for a weekend visit, but his parents are the first to acknowledge that he seems to be invigorated by the change in lifestyle. He is adamant that his work is 'no problem', and when he goes back on the Sunday evening they feel a little more relaxed about him. They also feel happier about his younger brother, Gary, who has spent more time at home during the past few weeks than he has for several months. He has been keenly embarrassed by his brother's behaviour and goes to great pains to discourage his friends from calling. This is another source of grief to his mother, as she has always enjoyed having young people around the house. Because they cannot give Gary any explanation or reassurance about his brother's behaviour, the parents tend to avoid the subject altogether, but they are only too aware of their younger son's anger and distress.

Perhaps we should not be surprised to learn that half-way through the term, Steven's course tutor has written to the local authority's grants section to say that he has not attended one lecture or handed in a single piece of work since his return to college; he has been warned that this cannot continue. Meanwhile, the college welfare officer rings the parents to tell them that it seems that Steven only went along for his first injection and has not been seen at the doctor's surgery since.

By the time his parents rush up to visit him, Steven may have realized he must do something and is now attending the occasional (afternoon) lecture. He greets his parents pleasantly and quickly tells them he has now had his injection. He seems to be rather better than they expected, and provides coffee and biscuits for his visitors. They can only stay for just over an hour, and on the journey back they marvel at the way Steven has coped with what must have been a stressful visit. They suddenly wonder if he can in fact assume 'normality' for such a short time, when needs be.

Predictably, the situation quickly deteriorates, and Steven's parents are eventually asked to collect their son from college. They are shocked when they see him; he has probably not washed for days and is unshaven. His clothes are crumpled and grubby and his eyes have a glazed, wild look about them.

FURTHER BREAKDOWN

Back home, they find he is neither eating nor sleeping and keeps muttering to himself for no apparent reason. They telephone the hospital and are told to contact the GP if they need help. The doctor suggests they bring Steven to the surgery, but the latter adamantly refuses to cooperate in this. He screams at them that they are trying to put him away. For the first time, they sense real fear in their son, and his wild, tortured expression makes them very frightened for him. The GP insists that Steven must come to see him; he cannot force his attentions on a patient. Once again the parents are at a loss to know what to do. During the next two days the situation worsens to the point that they dare not let Steven out of their sight. This time his father phones the hospital and demands to speak to his son's psychiatrist. He has to content himself with speaking to a secretary, who explains that the psychiatrist can make a visit to the patient's home, but only if the GP requests this. Armed with this information, Steven's father is able to instigate such a visit, which eventually takes place a further two days later. By this time both parents are seemingly nervous wrecks; they have arranged for Gary to stay with a friend throughout this crisis, but they themselves have had no such reprieve. Their elder son now walks around the house clutching a bread knife, for protection, he tells them.

The psychiatrist quickly decides that Steven needs to come into hospital, but the young man is adamant that he is not 'going in one of those places again', nor is he prepared to have an injection or take the tablets that have been prescribed. So the psychiatrist tells the parents that he is arranging for an approved social worker to call and assess Steven so that an application can be made for his formal admission to hospital under the Mental Health Act 1983. Later, the psychiatrist goes outside to meet and talk with the social worker. Steven immediately starts threatening his parents and accusing them of trying to get rid of him and throwing him to the wolves. In the ensuing chaos, they are too confused to even begin to understand why a *social worker* is coming to assess Steven when his hospital doctor, and now his GP, are both certain he should be in hospital. As the psychiatrist drives away to his next visit, the social worker comes into the house and speaks briefly with the parents and their son. She suggests politely that his mother and father calm down and stop trying to speak for Steven. The latter is now inexplicably quiet and rational and the young woman suggests he should go and talk with her in another room. The parents watch in amazement as their son civilly agrees and pleasantly shows her into the dining-room. They come out fifteen minutes or so later and the social worker tells Steven's parents that she agrees with him that he does not need to go into hospital. However, she feels he should have a break from home during the daytime and she will arrange for him to attend the local day centre.

His mother protests almost hysterically, asking if she *understands*. Does she know what has been happening, does she know two doctors think he should be in hospital, does she know that Steven won't go to the day centre? Steven shrugs his shoulders and mutters, 'You see?', and the social worker nods, telling him she will call back as soon as she can arrange a place at the day centre later in the week. She leaves, and at this point Steven's mother sinks into a chair and her whole body shakes with heartbroken sobs. For the first time in months, her son moves towards her with loving concern and begs her, 'Don't do that, Mum, please don't do that!'

His father feels an overwhelming rage: how can everyone forsake them in this way, how can his brave, cheerful wife be driven to this, and how can anyone fail to see that her first-born son is so sick? He rushes round to the GP's surgery and demands to see him immediately; he is slightly mollified when the doctor seems to be nearly as angry as himself at the news. He quietly curses a system which insists on a 'non-medic' deciding whether or not someone should be formally admitted to hospital, and which even puts pressure on that officer to avoid such admission whenever suitable alternatives can be found. '*What* alternatives?' shouts the enraged father. 'He won't go to the day centre, when the time comes, and anyway what do we do in the meantime?' The doctor nods in agreement and says that some of his colleagues are starting to take such patients off their registers when this sort of situation occurs, as the system renders them powerless to care for their interests any longer. He knows Steven can now only deteriorate until such time as someone can get some medication into him; the family must contact him again if they get any more desperate, and perhaps another social worker will see the situation differently . . .

Without any respite or sleep, that night and the next day seem an eternity to these desperate parents. The following night, despite their determination to keep an eye on their son at all times, both eventually drop off to sleep just before dawn, exhausted from their continuing ordeal. Steven immediately slips out of the house, and they are rudely awakened an hour or so later by the shrill call of the telephone. The police have picked him up walking down the middle of the main road leading out of town, wearing only his pyjamas and clutching a bread knife to his chest. It was a miracle that he was not killed, his parents are told, but he has now been admitted to hospital.

LIGHT AT THE END OF THE TUNNEL

When Steven's father telephones the hospital, he is told that his son has been medicated and is now sleeping peacefully. At this point the father is overcome with emotion and relief. In tears, he hugs his wife and tells her, 'This time we'll get some answers, I promise you.' When they are both rested, he rings back to the hospital and asks for an appointment with Steven's psychiatrist; once more a private interview is refused, but, they are told, he would be happy for the parents to come along to the ward-round tomorrow.

Just before the ward-round starts next morning, Steven's parents have a few words with their son who has already lost the wild look of the past week. He is quite calm and does not seem to mind at all being back in hospital. He cannot remember how he got there, but does not seem too concerned about this. He is so drowsy that they assume he is heavily medicated. A nurse asks the three of them to come and join the psychiatrist and the staff team. When they walk into the crowded room, Steven's mother gives a little gasp of shock. She cannot begin to imagine who all these people can be; surely they don't have to talk with the doctor in front of all these strangers? Unhappily she is wrong about that, and the exhausted woman is conscious only of a sea of strange faces all seemingly staring at her. She gradually becomes aware that several people are addressing questions to Steven, who is understandably rather vague and disjointed in his answers. Much to her relief, Steven is sent back to the ward after a few minutes, and the psychiatrist inquires if the parents have any questions to ask.

Any questions to ask? Where on earth should they start, they wonder? Finally Steven's father gets a grip of himself and manages, 'What is wrong with the boy?' Inexplicably, the doctor acts as if that was not the sort of question that was expected, but after a seemingly long silence he tells them, 'It does rather look as though Steven may have a schizophrenic illness.' Both his parents flinch as if they have been struck; that dreadful word that no one can spell or pronounce, which seems to be mentioned only in horrific scandals reported in the press! Suddenly they realize that the doctor is speaking again, suggesting that they have a word with the hospital social worker after the ward-round, if they want to know more about this type of illness. Steven's mother is not at all sure she wants anything more to do with social workers, but she glances at her husband, who nods. Eventually she manages to ask, 'Will my son get better?' After another pause the doctor tells her that they hope so, but Steven will need a lot of help and may have to take medication indefinitely. Hopelessly intimidated by the presence of all these strangers seemingly staring at them expectantly, and not really able to comprehend any more what is happening, the boy's parents decline to ask any more questions and they wait with their son in the ward for the social worker to join them. Later, this young man takes the parents away to his office and over a cup of coffee apologizes for the ordeal they have just had to face: 'We all know how visitors must feel when they come in and join us in the ward-round, but no one seems able to devise a better system!' Realizing they are feeling more relaxed now, the social worker invites them to tell him what they do know about schizophrenia. On discovering that this amounts to nothing of any significance, he gives them a leaflet that explains the basic features of the illness. He asks them if they would like to be put in touch with a self-help group. This turns out to be the local branch of the National Schizophrenia Fellowship and it seems that relatives of sufferers meet regularly to discuss common problems and ways of dealing with them. The group will also be able to recommend books and papers dealing with the subject in a simple, straightforward manner. Before they leave, the social worker explains about disability benefits and tells them how to go about protecting Steven's rights in this direction. They appreciate this; no such advice had been offered when he was in hospital before. By the time they arrive home, both parents are beginning to come to terms with the fearful-sounding diagnosis. At least they now know the nature of the beast that has been destroying their family's happiness! They had not been able to fight an invisible enemy, but now they feel they have a chance, and they intend to find out everything they can to help their elder son.

Before very long they meet other families who have been down the same road and survived with varying degrees of success. They learn something of the sorts of things that will have been happening to their son in his private nightmare world. They realize that his hostility will have been provoked by paranoid ideas that have no basis in reality. All this enables them to understand a little better why they have not been able to find any way to help Steven up to now.

In the next six weeks or so, Steven's health steadily improves and he becomes stabilized on a slightly different drug, which makes him less drowsy than the one previously prescribed. The parents once more see a dramatic improvement in their son, but this time it seems set to last and they are now realizing that the nightmare is beginning to recede. They are surprised that Steven still seems to have learned nothing about his illness, but perhaps they will be able to share with him some of the things they have discovered as time goes on? They have been warned several times that the way back will be long and arduous. However, they are now beginning to believe that their elder son may eventually find some contentment and that their house may sometimes resound with his laughter once more. Already Gary is starting to bring his friends home again and, as he learns about Steven's illness, so the younger boy is showing his eagerness to make allowances and to meet his brother more than half-way.

It looks as if this family may have found a way forward at last; Steven may be one of the lucky ones. He has survived several situations when his life may well have been in danger, and he is gradually regaining his grip on reality. What has he been experiencing throughout the desperate past few years?

A PSYCHOTIC NIGHTMARE

One sunny October afternoon in 1985 found Steven restlessly watching the clock as he waited for the bell that would signal the end of the lesson. His mind was on the extra practice game at 4 pm in preparation for Saturday's important fixture with the school from the other side of town. He had several ideas he was anxious to put to the others and had lost interest in what was going on in the classroom, when he suddenly became aware of the physics teacher looking at him, and experienced an inexplicable feeling of guilt and furtiveness. Glancing back at the teacher, Steven could see that he was aware that something was wrong by the way he stared back at him. The boy felt himself becoming hot and uncomfortable with an overwhelming sensation of guilt and shame. When the longed-for end of lesson arrived, instead of feeling relieved and glad to get away, the captain of the school's 'B' soccer team felt he owed the class teacher some sort of apology and muttered something unintelligible before rushing past him self-consciously. Steven's misery stayed with him throughout the practice session, and when he attempted to explain his planned strategy for Saturday's game, he could see his team-mates glancing at each other in embarrassment. Suddenly realizing that they were aware of his guilt and whatever the reasons for it, he gave up the attempt to share his ideas and tried instead to throw himself into the game. He was partially successful in this, but horribly aware of his each and every movement and the attention this seemed to attract from the rest of the team. Much to the surprise of one or two close friends, he could not get away from the changing-rooms quickly enough and left for home on his own.

Steven had plenty of time over the coming weeks to try to understand what had happened. To start with he could make no sense of it at all; every time he tried he came back again to that moment in the classroom when he knew that something dreadful had happened and that it concerned him. He had immediately discovered that the teacher was aware of this and, before very long, his team-mates as well; they said nothing, but he could tell from the way they looked at him. Later he had found that it was the same with his other friends, the rest of the school staff, and even with his family. Perhaps it was the level of shame he felt that memorable first afternoon which made him understand that whatever had happened – *whatever he had done or been responsible for* – was so appalling that others were too embarrassed to mention it. Certainly, even those nearest and dearest to him were aware of his guilt but did not refer to the matter. He was deeply hurt as well as mortified; how dreadful to be such an embarrassment to your friends and family that they won't even discuss your agony with you! Quickly he cursed himself for even thinking like that; he knew it was a shameful attitude, and it just showed how evil he had become that he was now feeling resentful towards those who would be most affected, even humiliated, by his behaviour.

Before long, Steven could no longer stand the curious, even reproachful looks from his friends, and he went to great efforts to avoid them. He backed out of the soccer team, telling the games master he was worried about the extra amount of work he had to cover for his 'A' levels. He withdrew from his club badminton team with the same explanation, but offered none to his friends as they would already know why he was not good enough to mix with ordinary people any more. For a while, he was puzzled as to why they still called at his home, but made no attempt to go and talk to them as he did not want pity and could not stand to see it in their faces. He found that he now tended to avoid eye contact with others anyway, perhaps because he was frightened of seeing the truth about himself reflected back to him.

As Steven became more and more isolated and unhappy, he was aware of others muttering about him and referring to him in their seemingly innocent conversation. For this reason, being in a room with more than one other person became an ordeal, and never more so than when his father and Gary were together. He had to acknowledge that they might well be more embarrassed by his behaviour than most, but did so wish they would not signify to each other in so many hurtful ways what they felt about him. His father regularly tapped his foot when he wished to convey something about his elder son, and Gary would nod and mutter just softly enough for his brother to miss what was said. Try as he would, Steven could not quite see Gary's lips moving or catch the gist of what he was saying. Steven increasingly sought out his mother for company, given that she was on her own, but resented her nearly as much as the others for being two-faced about him. It was only when she was alone with him that she seemed to relax and not resent his presence. Several times he invited her to talk about her disappointment in him; several times he opened with 'I know what you think', or 'I do understand', but she feigned ignorance and exasperation when he did this rather than responding honestly. He gave up on this, feeling sick and empty inside.

As time went on he realized that his crime was such that it was not something that anyone could acknowledge openly. What could be done about it then? Society had ways of dealing with people who were dreadfully anti-social. How would they punish him? Was he to be poisoned to death? He sometimes felt *so ill*, so tired and weak, although he had given up all the exercise he used to do. His GP did not seem interested, but did tell him to come back if things did not improve. So each time he went to see him, Steven was able to mention all the physical problems he was having, like his chronic constipation, and his feeling that he was going to choke when he attempted to sleep. He did not trust the doctor enough to tell him that he lay in bed for hours at night certain that he would die or be murdered in his sleep; the doctor might be part of the conspiracy to do away with him. This seemed even probable when the GP told him one Saturday that he and his mother were both worried about him as he did not seem to be the happy and fit boy that he used to be; he would like Steven to see a psychiatrist. That was it; they were going to lock him away and hide the key!

In the event, it seemed that the psychiatrist must have heard of his predicament and realized that he did not need psychiatric treatment. Very much relieved, Steven was nevertheless disappointed that the man did not attempt to rescue him in some way, by insisting that he have a thorough physical examination, for example. Still, he was probably no more interested in protecting the young man from his sins than the rest of society. Meanwhile, Steven was becoming increasingly resentful that his parents were being so devious; they kept expressing concern for him and even seeking help, while talking audibly on other occasions about his being evil and the shame he had brought on them. Whenever he challenged them about this, hoping to bring the ghastly truth out into the open, they feigned ignorance and even astonishment.

All in all, it came as a relief to be able to get away from everyone he knew when the time came to go to college. The only refuge he had found during the past unhappy months had been his schoolwork, though most of this was done in the comparative peace and quiet of the school library, while avoiding formal lessons, or in his room during the restless night-time hours. This had paid off and he suspected he had achieved better examination results than if he had been free to live his previous lifestyle. However, when he moved into his digs and prepared to start his new life far away from home, Steven found himself scared as he had never been before. He missed the safety of his room at home and the knowledge that he could have a few minutes' relative peace with his mother whenever the stress threatened to overcome him. He knew no one here although he would not wish to change that anyway; everyone and everything seemed to pose a threat to the terrified young man. Somehow he could not find the strength to go to more than the first few college lectures. Each time he returned to his room wringing-wet with sweat and emotionally exhausted. He did not hear a word that was said anyway and he was finding it increasingly hard to organize himself or even to wake up for the morning sessions. He was not eating properly and only felt safe venturing out in the evenings when it was dark.

That was the case, anyhow, until he realized that the drivers of all passing white cars were keeping an eye on him in his digs. At last he knew the nature of his crime. The more he thought about it, the more certain he became that he had let his country down in some way; perhaps he was a spy and guilty of treason? That would explain why he was being watched – perhaps the white cars were from a foreign embassy? Initially he was able to deal with this to some extent by closing the curtains of his room during the day. However, his landlady did not seem to like this habit and was also starting to probe him about his lack of activity during the day and asking why he did not keep any food in the fridge. She pretended to be concerned, but Steven was not fooled, and sure enough one day she brought a doctor to see him in his room. This was a familiar scene, with a doctor trying to pretend that he was a psychiatric case once again. He wanted Steven to go into hospital or to take some tablets (was he from the same country as the car drivers?) In desperation, Steven assured the doctor that he'd be fine; of course he'd take the tablets and come and see him in a week's time. The doctor left. A few evenings later Steven slipped out of the house to walk in the comforting quiet of the night and try to relax enough to work out what he must do next. Suddenly he realized that in the darkness he could not see which of the passing cars were the dreaded white ones; in a blind panic he started to run and left the road as soon as he could. He found himself in a large open space and fled to the far corner, crouching by a hedge as he heard a car approaching. He was not really surprised when uniformed men jumped out . . .

IN CONCLUSION

From this point when the police took him to the local psychiatric hospital, it should not be difficult to surmise how things appeared to the troubled young man over the following months. For a very brief period the nightmare started to recede, but he had been given no explanations for what had happened to him, so he had no means by which to separate reality from fantasy. He had no way of understanding, therefore, that he had done nothing wrong; no way of appreciating that no one had been plotting against him and that he was hallucinating when he heard his parents cursing him and Gary muttering about him. He had no way of knowing that an illness had caused all his misery. Without such explanations for Steven and for those close to him, and without a longer period of relief from his symptoms, the prognosis had to be poor. In the event, all the terrors and delusions would return and there would be yet further pain and danger before this intelligent young man would have the chance to understand and come to terms with his experiences; experiences typical of those of many young people I have known during the past seventeen years.

The next chapter will take a look at the symptoms that are so characteristic of a schizophrenic illness and what we know and understand about them. Meanwhile, perhaps it might be worth while pausing for a moment to consider; if Steven was your son, would you feel that his and your interests had been well served?

*

Author's note: Steven is a fictional character who closely resembles several of the young people I have worked with over the past seventeen years and whose experiences are typical of many, many more. Nevertheless, the rest of the case studies in this book are of individuals who are well known to me. Unimportant details have been changed to ensure that each one's identity is protected.

2 · What Happens in Schizophrenia?

The strange and frightening ideas that Steven experienced are typical of a classic cluster of symptoms which we call acute schizophrenia. It is interesting that most of these bizarre symptoms have been described in exactly similar terms by sufferers from different cultures all over the world. Despite predictable variations in the course and severity of each individual's illness, it is notable that schizophrenia sufferers do report similar experiences and also make strikingly similar interpretations about what is happening to them.

There are three main strands to this type of schizophrenic illness and these are *altered perception, thought disorder* and *delusional ideas*, the last perhaps best described as fixations which are patently false and impervious to reasoned argument. As these are probably provoked by, and certainly aided and abetted by, *altered perception*, let us take a look at this phenomenon first. Any or all of the five senses may become distorted or actually relay faulty messages, as happens when the individual is hallucinating.

HEARING

The sufferer's hearing may become distorted and acutely sensitive, with sounds becoming piercingly high-pitched or deafening in volume. More confusingly, the individual can be bombarded with stimuli from all sides, unable to *select out* the background noises in the way we normally do. For example, attempts to take part in a conversation with another person can be sabotaged by the background noises such as distant traffic or birds singing becoming as penetrating as the voice at one's side. The sufferer's ears may pick up dozens of sounds which would normally go unnoticed.

Possibly the most disturbing symptoms of this illness are the *auditory hallucinations* so many experience. These are sounds which are not there but which are heard by the individual concerned. These sounds may take the form of music, humming, mutterings or laughter, but more commonly a 'voice' or 'voices' will be heard. Importantly, these sounds are *heard* and not imagined. We do not know the mechanism behind this phenomenon but it is real enough to throw its victims into confusion and despair. In some cases, a voice or voices will talk to, or at, them, often jeeringly and using the sort of language that many find too embarrassing to repeat out loud. For others, the voice or voices may be the type that carries on a running commentary on their thoughts or on everything that is going on around them. The voice or voices may constantly issue instructions, sometimes exhorting the individual to do something self-destructive, and unless this can be resisted the results can be maiming or even fatal. Carol North, now a practising psychiatrist, has written a clear and fascinating account of the many years of torment she spent with such voices as her constant companions.[1] These sorts of voice are usually recognized as some sort of phenomenon sooner or later, and the individual may eventually mention or acknowledge the torment. Sometimes, too, a voice is eventually perceived by a sufferer as his or her own thoughts being spoken aloud, and such an explanation naturally brings with it a certain amount of relief.

More dangerous, and very common, is the experience of hearing the familiar voices of loved ones, or of other people *who matter*, talking about the individual in the third person, usually in condemning terms. Imagine for a moment the effect this would be likely to have on sufferers already becoming isolated in a world of confusion and suspicion. They have no way of knowing that their senses are playing tricks on them; no way of appreciating that the people these voices seem to belong to are not in fact offending in this way. As we have seen, sufferers may believe that they are guilty of some awful wrongdoing; it is only a short step to fearing that those who matter most – *those they need most* – will turn away from them. They have no way of knowing that the familiar voices talking about them so disparagingly are not real; that they are remarkable phenomena and also manifestations of their own fears. Perhaps the experience of one young woman will illustrate the perils of this type of symptom.

After two years of unrelieved and undiagnosed symptoms, Pat started to believe that she had somehow made her mother fatally ill and that her father hated her for this. Such was the strength of this conviction, that she used to 'hear' her warm and caring father planning to do away with her, and her supposedly sick mother protesting, but gradually agreeing Pat must go. For months this tortured girl walked the house at night listening to her parents (actually asleep, or anxiously listening to their daughter's restless movements) planning her demise. Eventually, by the time she was admitted to hospital, Pat would not stay alone in the same house with her father, so sure was she that he would kill her and that she was deserving of such a fate. Months later, when Pat was on her way to a real recovery and gradually learning to believe in her parents' love for her again, the psychiatrist asked her why she hadn't mentioned long ago that she was 'hearing voices'. This intelligent girl suggested, by way of reply, that if she had *known* she was hearing voices, much of her misery could have been alleviated! As it happened, Pat began to question her own senses while still in hospital, when she continued to hear her parents talking about her in the middle of the night, although she knew them to be miles away at home. Later, as the medication began to take effect, she began to tighten her grasp on reality. She was eventually helped to discuss her experiences with her parents, which in turn enabled them to help Pat appreciate when her senses were playing tricks on her. Gradually the voices started to recede, but it was a very long time before she was completely free of them and of their power instantly to undermine her returning confidence.

Others do not necessarily have the benefit of such insight, and it is not uncommon for patients to be discharged from hospital without they or their families learning about these false messages that had already caused so much distrust and hostility. Sufferers innocently deny 'hearing voices', because they do not know that their senses have been playing tricks on them. This means that they try to pick up the thread of their previous lives believing that the seeming betrayal of their loved ones was part of their 'sentence' for being evil. This is not a promising foundation on which to maintain a hold on reality and rebuild valued relationships and trust.

VISION

As with the sense of hearing, vision can become acutely sensitive, with colours seeming too vivid, as in a badly tuned television. Alternatively, everything can be perceived as a dull greyish colour and this is often a depressive feature. Similarly, confused sufferers may complain of other exaggerations such as everyone they have seen that day looking incredibly beautiful or frighteningly ugly.

Brian is a young man who has been plagued with symptoms that make objects, creatures and people appear to change shape, and facial features become distorted. He has never managed to resume anything approaching a normal lifestyle since his long-delayed diagnosis several years ago. Most of his continuing distress revolves around his distorted vision. On occasion he is free of symptoms other than this particular one of experiencing the faces around him changing shape and colour, sometimes becoming comical and at other times grotesque. It took some time for him to be able to explain just how terrifying he finds this; he interprets the fact that such things are able to happen as proof that some evil omnipotent being is present. The fact that such phenomena are clearly distracting scarcely seems to matter to him; it is his interpretation of the meaning behind them that he finds so chilling. Many is the time I have seen him glance anxiously at the faces around him and settle back relaxed for a few moments when all was apparently as it should be. Talking about these feelings and discussion about the eye and its intricate delicacy would reassure him for an hour or so, but the terror always returned, stopping this pleasant and previously sociable young man from venturing out of his home alone.

Rather differently, some sufferers have problems with judging distance, speed and size. We all take these remarkable skills for granted, but without them crossing a busy road can become a mammoth task. For some individuals, difficulties with judging distance seem to be all part of a 'blurring' of their own boundaries, and they may unwittingly move up too close to others, invading their personal 'space' and so making them feel uneasy. Sadly, such action can be misinterpreted as aggressive or sexually provocative behaviour.

Another particularly worrying symptom experienced by many sufferers is the inability to know whether or not others are looking at them. This leads to ideas that they are being constantly watched and clearly contributes to considerable discomfort and paranoid beliefs.

Visual hallucinations are far less common than auditory ones, but they can range from flashing lights and fleeting shadows through to the seeing of ghosts or spirits. Some sufferers believe these latter experiences to be of a religious origin, even perhaps a visitation from God. Where this is seen as something rare and precious, it can lead to a new or revived interest in religion, clearly a positive feature in a changed lifestyle. But others interpret such an experience as confirmation of their imagined guilt and an indication that they have been singled out for some wrongdoing. Jean, a housewife and mother, experienced a 'visitation' not long after her first breakdown in 1968. From that moment, she has believed that her illness is some terrible vengeance because she had had a couple of wartime love affairs before she married her husband. This caring, conscientious woman is constantly persecuted by such thoughts, and the protests of her family and friends are entirely ignored. The common delusion about having sinned in some way has been confirmed for her by this visual experience, and she believes she is damned forever in the eyes of God and that she has been singled out for punishment.

TOUCH

Some sufferers find their sense of touch plays tricks on them. Their skin may feel 'creepy', tingle or become ultra-sensitive, particularly on the sexual areas of the body. They may believe others are touching them, leading to ideas of being indecently assaulted or 'invaded' in some way.

More generally, surfaces of objects can 'feel wrong'; a smooth, flat table-top feeling furry or three-dimensional, for example.

SMELL

It is not unusual for sufferers to experience aromas that are not there. These hallucinations are sometimes quite pleasing in that the individual may smell exquisite perfumes or tropical flowers. Sometimes they are less so, bringing noxious smells such as those of faeces.

Again, this sense may be greatly heightened as well as distorted in this illness, which can lead to some individuals being acutely aware of their own body odour and convinced, therefore, that everyone else finds them objectionable. Not quite so agonizing for one sufferer – Tony – is his awareness of other people's odour and his conviction that his family do not have high enough standards of hygiene; he continually urges them to take baths, while showing little concern about his own personal habits!

TASTE

It is common for sufferers, when quite ill, to find that everything tastes odd; they usually complain that foods and drinks taste bitter, or coppery, and this understandably contributes to paranoid ideas about being poisoned. We rely mainly on our senses of taste and smell to confirm that the food we eat is what we believe it to be.

ANOTHER ALTERED PERCEPTION

As we have noted, all five senses are likely to fail sufferers in their attempts to make sense of their surroundings. This can be a gradual, destructive process that tends to nullify everything they have previously understood about the world around them. One more important distortion that is both quite common and disruptive in schizophrenia is the individual's perception of *time*. On the one hand, this can seem to literally 'stand still', and a few minutes can be experienced as an eternity. On the other, time can seem to race past in a way that makes the individual anxious and frightened.

Rather differently, some individuals become obsessed with another time in history, and believe they are part of it; they may surround themselves with the music and fashions, for example, of this previous age or a future one as in science fiction.

A more frustrating confusion with time is provoked by the upturning of the body's normal 'twenty-four-hour clock'. In many cases of schizophrenia, this clock goes 'into reverse'. When this happens, the individual needs to sleep when everyone is up and about and, conversely, to remain wide awake at night when the rest of the world is sleeping. The sufferer may sleep or be weighed down with a really exhausting lethargy all day, only to come to life around late evening, feeling relatively lively throughout most of the night. This can be an enormous obstacle to resuming a normal lifestyle and can also have a very adverse effect on the rest of the household's sleep.

ABNORMAL THOUGHT STRUCTURE

One common way for sufferers to experience this is to feel that they are no longer in control of their own thoughts. One writer comments: 'Instead of being guided along a chain of associations, the patient's thought proceeds independently. Mental activity becomes haphazard as thoughts take on a life of their own, replacing the person's intention'.[2] An alarming prospect, and one that understandably provokes delusional ideas that others are putting thoughts into one's head.

Some individuals are tormented by unwelcome *intrusive thoughts* which tend to 'churn round in their mind' with an alarming intensity. Perhaps less distressing, but nevertheless potentially embarrassing, is the common experience of 'mind-blocking', bringing claims from affected individuals that their thoughts have been taken away from them. When one suspects that such forces are at work, it is a small step to believing that others can read your mind and that your thoughts are being broadcast for all to hear; a particularly sobering idea.

So one of the common features in a schizophrenic illness is that the individual's thoughts can flit from one subject to another or can focus and become trapped on one topic or word, rather as happens when a record becomes cracked, or can become a total blank; all without any apparent rhyme or reason. In much the same way that one's thoughts can 'take on a life of their own', so it seems can the attention span. Normally, our attention span is governed by our glancing around us at one thing after another until such time as we find what we are looking for, or notice something that interests us. Some schizophrenia sufferers find that they no longer have control over this process. Instead of being able to shift their attention from one thing to another in this way, it seems to act independently of its owner and comes to rest wherever it feels so inclined. They find their attention riveted on some apparently insignificant object, unable to move away from it. When experiencing this 'capture of attention',[3] they may be mesmerized by something – a stapler in a colleague's hand, for example – and are unable to move on to other things. Such a phenomenon could well explain many sufferers' insistence that everything has a special meaning in this illness. This *heightened significance* may apply to a seemingly unimportant object, a word, a person, or a colour, with everything 'yellow', for example, assuming importance. It often applies, too, to an idea, and indeed it is quite common for sufferers to claim that they have suddenly found the meaning to life; all is revealed to them. One has explained:

I was suddenly confronted with an overwhelming conviction that I had discovered the secrets of the universe, which were being rapidly made plain with incredible lucidity. . . . I had no sense of doubt or the awareness of the possibility of doubt.[4]

Rather sadly, such inspiration is not maintained when good health returns. Those sufferers whose 'discoveries' have seemed to them to be of such consequence that they have felt bound to record them at the time, are usually disappointed when well again. They find they have written down a collection of words that seem to be saying nothing in particular, that no longer reveal whatever *meaning* they once had.

DELUSIONAL THINKING

Convictions that one's thoughts are being controlled, that all sorts of insignificant objects have a special meaning, and that the secrets of the universe can be revealed in a moment's inspiration, are clearly part of the delusional thinking that is an integral part of a schizophrenic illness. Having a clear appreciation of the out-of-the-ordinary experiences that lead to such false beliefs makes it easier to understand why its victims have these convictions. If we pause and consider all the tricks that the senses may be playing upon the brains of individuals developing this illness, we may be less surprised at the sorts of idea that they express. It seems reasonable to assume that human life as we understand it depends on the brain *making sense* of all the messages reaching it. If delusional thinking is the natural result of the brain trying to create order out of an escalating chaos, then this would explain the remarkable constancy of content in schizophrenic delusions, with so many sufferers finding such similar explanations for what is happening to them. For those who are tormented by distorted feelings of guilt for being 'evil' (a word frequently used by such individuals in connection with themselves), it is a short step to feeling that they should and will be persecuted in some way. When they talk of their experiences in retrospect, sufferers frequently speak of being watched by pilots from airplanes or helicopters or by drivers of passing cars. They speak of fears of being captured for interrogation, or refer to being poisoned by radiation through the walls or water-pipes of their seemingly safe home. Some believe they are being persecuted by Nazis, others that there is an immediate threat of nuclear war, and others, whose perception of time is awry, speak of invading Roman armies. In other words, as the perceived threat of danger escalates, paranoid sufferers may believe that the worst horrors appropriate to their particular culture are about to descend upon them.

Many sufferers pointedly avoid listening to the radio or watching television, although this may have been a favourite occupation for them in the past. This avoidance behaviour is often a sign that they are having *ideas of reference*, in which they believe that everything happening on the programme is to do with them. This frightening phenomenon can be experienced in two ways: either the participants in the programme, and particularly news announcers, actually talk to or about the sufferer (who is hearing voices), or the content of the programme seems to refer to him or her. It is an indication of how real and distressing such an experience can be that many sufferers then deprive themselves completely of these popular forms of entertainment. Similar ideas can be experienced in other situations, with individuals believing that everyone present is plotting against them. This can be confirmed by someone scratching his nose, or tapping his foot, or by any other common-place movement or action perceived as a message which everyone else understands. In much the same way, the talk all around the sufferer in a crowd – in a supermarket or at a football match, for example – may be interpreted as 'double-talk' containing messages about him or her. These ideas cause acute distress and I have seen a young man in tears after leaving a supermarket where two girls at the till made remarks that were clearly harmless, free of malice and bearing no reference to him.

Some sufferers are tormented by *delusions of omnipotence*, in which they believe that they have undue influence on the people and events around them. These can be the opposite side of the coin to ideas that one's thoughts are being controlled, with individuals claiming that they know what others are thinking or are about to say because they can control their thoughts and actions. Such ideas are common, even in timid and frightened individuals such as Brian, whom we discussed earlier. Again, such ideas can lead to escalating feelings of guilt as the individual becomes convinced that he or she is responsible for everything that goes wrong, even for large-scale disasters. Other *grandiose* ideas sometimes lead to sufferers claiming to be famous personalities, such as dictators or saints, and there is one delightful story of a very sick man indignantly telling a fellow patient that he was an impostor as they couldn't both be Jesus Christ! Again, for sufferers who are convinced that they have heard God speaking to them and who believe that they have discovered the meaning of the universe, such assumptions about identity may seem to be reasonable.

Delusions about religious matters are very common in schizo-phrenia, so much so that they are very often the central feature of any one individual's illness. Sadly, in paranoid schizophrenia, this can lead to convictions of eternal damnation, with hours being spent each day searching the Bible for evidence of forgiveness. It is a pity that Church leaders rarely have an opportunity to learn about the significance of this type of symptom as such knowledge could help to alleviate the misery for some individuals.

Another very common symptom is a preoccupation with sexual matters. This may manifest itself as a confusion over sexual identity, with, for example, heterosexual individuals becoming convinced during their illness that they are homosexual. Some male sufferers are tortured by guilt because of sexual fantasies they claim are inserted into their thoughts and which they cannot control; another source of self-condemnation. Female sufferers may complain they have been assaulted or interfered with during their sleep. Others make unreal claims about a non-existent sex life. One psychiatrist comments:

The number of delusional ideas about sex found among schizophrenics is impressive. I have one patient who regularly announces that she is pregnant although she has not had intercourse. Another claims she has been continuously pregnant for five years and may deliver any week.[5]

Delusions about the body in general are very common and it is not unknown for extremely sick sufferers to complain they have been invaded and have another life inside them. Others claim that their muscles are wasting away or that their brain is melting. One young woman I know was certain her voice had been changed and she could not understand why others would not acknowledge this.

Some sufferers complain of all sorts of physical ailments, particularly when they are first developing a schizophrenic illness. This is often dismissed as hypochondriacal behaviour, particularly as there are frequently irrational fears of dying from cancer or some such dreaded disease. We can almost certainly find the origins of such beliefs in the torturous fears of some individuals, but some in fact are clearly physically as well as mentally ill. By the time of their breakdown, many individuals are painfully underweight, have an unnatural pallor and glazed eyes, and may be suffering from pronounced allergies. Most of them appreciate by this time that they are ill, and feel very unwell indeed. Unfortunately they only recognize (and perhaps magnify) their *physical* frailty, often believing that they have been poisoned or in some way made fatally ill by their persecutors. By this time they will almost certainly reject any suggestion that they might need psychiatric treatment. This determined denial of mental illness is, perhaps, the core of all the delusional thinking in schizophrenia. It is a tragic irony that the brain's successful rationalization of all the false messages reaching it may finally preclude any recognition by the individual that the torment has been caused by the symptoms of a treatable illness.

FEATURES WORTH NOTING

One very frequent physical feature in acute schizophrenia is an inability to *make eye contact* with the other person. Individuals who experience this problem have difficulty in explaining it when they have recovered and there seem to be various possible reasons for a phenomenon that can be a real handicap to social functioning. Both an inability to determine whether one is being watched by others and/or the perceived risk of having one's attention 'captured' by their eyes might well play a part in this, but this is only speculation. The difficulty with making eye contact is so real that it is one of the few physical features that can be used as a measure of progress in those concerned; improved eye contact is indicative of returning good health. Meanwhile, it is not unknown for sufferers to find themselves being told to 'Look at me, please, when I'm speaking to you' by others who find their apparent lack of attention disconcerting.

More specifically, on rare occasions one comes across a gross speech defect which is resistant to any sort of therapy. If this dates back to a change of personality or behaviour, then it may be the only visible symptom of a schizophrenic illness. This was the case with Rita, a withdrawn young woman who had been a good mixer at school and keen on team sports. Gradually she gave up going out with her friends and later gave up her hobbies as well. As this coincided with the development of a severe stutter, this was seen to be the reason for her social withdrawal. Eventually she was offered speech therapy sessions but, instead of improving, the stuttering deteriorated to the point that every few words were punctuated by seemingly endless pauses. Rita gave up attempting conversation except when she was at home with her mother, and the latter soon complained that she could not move without her daughter at her side. Various mental health professionals in turn worked with Rita, several pronouncing her as 'attention-seeking' and 'manipulative'. When she was eventually admitted to a day hospital for two days a week, her extreme withdrawal behaviour was initially put down to her crippling speech defect. Later the mother was advised that her daughter would not get better unless they separated. While tentative plans were being made for Rita to move into a therapeutic community, she had to stay at home on her own for two days and nights while her mother went into hospital for an operation. The strain of this separation was enough for the young woman finally to break down, and she told her doctor of her convictions that she was being watched by the drivers of passing cars who were 'out to get her'. In retrospect, it became quite clear that Rita had exhibited several signs of a psychotic illness for some time. A prompt prescription of the appropriate medication quickly quietened her schizophrenic symptoms and *resolved her speech defect*. In the event, she was able to get on with her life, without the proposed residential placement, by persevering with a low dose of medication and learning all about her vulnerability.

As we have already noted, many of the physical changes in a schizophrenic breakdown are what might be expected in any serious illness. These may include extreme pallor, haggard features, staring, glazed eyes, loss of weight, disturbed sleeping patterns, constipation, interrupted menstrual pattern and eating disorders. More specifically, there is a substantial minority of sufferers who have an abnormally *raised pain threshold* and are notably insensitive to physical pain. This can be dangerous for such individuals as they rarely complain of discomfort that may indicate a serious developing disorder. Some of those sufferers who engage in horrendous self-mutilation fit into this category. They claim that such destructive acts cause little discomfort and bring relief from pent-up feelings of tension and frustration. Similarly, there is often little awareness of heat or cold in these individuals and it is not unusual to see them dressed quite inappropriately for the prevailing temperature.

Another visible feature of schizophrenia which can be seen in some individuals suffering an acute breakdown is the apparent sagging of the muscles and body frame, giving the impression that clothes are just *hanging* rather than actually being *worn* in the usual way. Bodily coordination seems to be faulty, especially, but not exclusively, in the chronic form of the illness. There is very often a jerky type of gait and shuffle that is instantly recognizable by those who have seen it before.

EATING DISORDER

One last feature of a developing schizophrenic illness is a pronounced eating disorder that very often accompanies the visible deterioration of the sufferer prior to diagnosis. Many sufferers develop abnormal cravings for sweet and stodgy foods, and their whole approach to food is quite remarkable. It sometimes seems that the more they eat of such foods, the more they resemble a starving animal pouncing on and devouring any available scraps. So intense is this craving in some individuals that it removes any semblance of civilized table manners and becomes a source of agonizing embarrassment to relatives and friends.

TWO DIFFERENT TYPES OF SYMPTOM

Until now we have looked at what can happen during, and leading up to, an acute schizophrenic breakdown. Several of the symptoms we have discussed, such as *ideas of reference*, can occur in other illnesses, and it is usually only when one finds a cluster of such symptoms together that the diagnosis is schizophrenia. All these strange and bizarre experiences are known as 'positive' symptoms and they are typical of those we associate with the acute form of this illness. Fortunately, they often respond well to medication and the prognosis can be good. They make up a very different picture to the 'negative' symptoms of schizophrenia, so named because they *take something away* from the individual's original personality. These are very much a feature of the chronic form of schizophrenia, but they can also play a part in an acute illness. Feelings of apathy and lethargy, difficulties with concentration, with making conversation and with socializing are examples of this type of illness. What effect may these 'negative' symptoms have on the everyday life of a sufferer?

It would be fair to say that a feeling of profound exhaustion is the underlying theme of a schizophrenic illness. The sufferer has little, if any, energy to spare and even less motivation to take on new ventures of any kind. Perhaps the nearest most of us get to experiencing this sort of lethargy and apathy is during the aftermath of a severe bout of influenza when we may feel lifeless and low, both mentally and physically. In the chronic form of schizophrenia, individuals seem constantly 'weighed down' with an overwhelming feeling of exhaustion. This is also very often a feature of the acute illness but gradually disappears with returning good health.

Sufferers may lose interest and pride in themselves. Many avoid looking in the mirror, do not bother to change their clothes, wash their hair or take regular showers or baths. This can be seen as asocial behaviour and becomes a source of friction between the apathetic sufferer and his or her family and friends.

LACK OF INTERESTS AND ACTIVITIES

Many sufferers lose interest in previously enjoyed activities and hobbies. Clearly, a lack of energy can explain this in part, but it goes further than this, with a tendency to spend day after day doing nothing at all. Apathy is as important as lethargy here and, as we have already noted, it is essential to work at trying to interest and motivate the individual to follow a routine of some sort, however modest this may be initially. There is no doubt that inactivity just breeds inactivity in this illness and becomes very detrimental for the sufferer. It does not help that the capacity for *concentration* is very limited. To read a page of a newspaper or a book can be a mammoth task when the senses may be bombarded with other distractions and when the attention may be 'captured' by one word or one line on the paper. Similarly, attempts to watch television or to participate in any social occasion can be sabotaged by difficulties in synchronizing the words that are spoken with what is happening visually. Most chronically ill sufferers can cope better if noise and activity are kept to a minimum, and speech confined to short, simple sentences which are spoken slowly. Similarly, one intelligent young man I know has found it helpful to borrow special *large print* books from the library; he finds this makes it easier to stay with the task in hand and is beginning, several months after his breakdown, to enjoy some light reading. Another helpful ploy can be to try re-reading old favourites from childhood, even comics, and some individuals find it helpful to revive their interest in television by rationing themselves to an occasional light comedy or soap opera they have enjoyed in the past. To achieve a half-hour's viewing without falling asleep or abandoning it half-way through is a good start! It is not too difficult to understand why some individuals find they cannot resist the ever-constant longing 'to switch off' and retire to bed when everyday living presents such challenges.

POVERTY OF SPEECH

This is probably the most common 'negative type' symptom and, quite simply, it is the inability to indulge in what we know as 'small talk'. It is almost impossible for sufferers so afflicted to initiate or take part in a conversation for the sake of it, and there can be no doubt that many individuals find this a crippling handicap which deters them from most social activities, including that of returning to or taking a job where there is a need to engage in these sort of niceties. The ability once more to engage in conversation does return as the illness wanes, but it remains a serious handicap for chronic sufferers.

BLUNTED AFFECT

A blunting of affect describes a reduced ability to *feel* things. Individuals complain they no longer feel any thrill of anticipation or excitement; they are aware of not really *enjoying* anything. It seems that everything has become dull and colourless, with none of the usual 'ups and downs' that provide the moments that matter, the highlights and the memories for the rest of us. Some sufferers who experience this deprivation complain that this is the biggest loss inflicted by their illness; they remember past feelings of excitement, anticipation and joy and appreciate all too well what they are missing.

Similar, and perhaps the most distressing personality change from the point of view of their loved ones, is the reduced ability in some individuals to feel emotionally about things that should matter to them. This has been very much overstated in the literature on schizophrenia, to the extent that there is a widespread belief that schizophrenia sufferers are self-absorbed to the point of not caring about the well-being of others. This is the reverse of the truth in many cases. However, a few are so distracted by their experiences in their fantasy world that they detach themselves from the extra stresses of the real world and others may not respond in the expected manner to news of joy or tragedy. Not only has the ability to feel been impaired to a greater or lesser extent, but, equally important, the social skills needed to deal with emotional situations may now also be lacking. *Blunting of affect*, incidentally, should not be confused with the much less common *incongruous affect* exhibited by some sufferers whose feelings appear to be out of step with their thoughts – the so-called 'split mind' that has led to all the confusion about the very rare and quite different 'Jekyll and Hyde' dual personality. This incongruous affect may be seen when an individual responds quite inappropriately, for example, giggling when given bad news.

MOOD CHANGE

Bearing in mind the heritage of disablement that some individuals are left with, it is not surprising that some suffer with a *reactive depression*. This is a predictable response to the tragic waste of potential which can result from this illness. This type of depression can pose a risk of suicide in those individuals who are recovering from a degree of illness that has damaged them enough to preclude any chance of resuming their previous lifestyle and who have enough insight left to realize this. Where the illness has damaged the personality, the loss is as real as it is for the athlete who loses a limb or the pianist who loses a hand. They have all lost a part of themselves and a part that has contributed to their lifestyle and their aspirations. The loss may be far more profound for those damaged permanently by schizophrenia as they have lost more than this; their experience of *themselves* may have changed. They have in effect lost the person they knew most intimately. This can be a real bereavement. Extra vigilance and encouragement from those around them are of vital importance at such a time, if an immediate risk of suicide is to be averted. Many are able eventually to come to terms with this loss if they are helped through this dangerous period of bereavement and painful adjustment.

Rather differently, there is a marked incidence of *clinical depression* in both the acute and chronic forms of schizophrenia. This type of depression is accompanied by clinical symptoms such as sleeplessness and loss of appetite, and is one that emanates from sickness in the body's chemistry rather than manifesting as a recognizable reaction to happenings in the individual's life or surroundings. When it is present in a schizophrenic illness, such depression seems to be very much part of the psychosis and tends to respond rather better to anti-psychotic medication than to anti-depressants. More rarely, there may be evidence of mood swings with signs of manic behaviour as well as depression.

VIOLENCE

Hopefully, this account of the sorts of torment and terror which can be experienced in schizophrenia will give some clues to the nature of the violent behaviour we sometimes read about when this illness hits the headlines. People with this illness tend to be over-sensitive and timid rather than aggressive; any violent behaviour is usually a response to some perceived threat of danger in the middle of a psychotic nightmare. It is more than likely to be in self-defence although it will seem to anyone unaware of the individual's inner psychotic nightmare to be unprovoked. Violent behaviour in this illness is almost always the result of unnoticed and untreated florid schizophrenic symptoms. There are in fact various tell-tale signs that someone is suffering in this way and Chapter 9 will take a look at some of these. Meanwhile, the increasing use of really bad language that is uncharacteristic in the individual concerned is one obvious sign of the escalating frustration and tension of a psychotic illness.

SUMMING UP

This chapter, then, has dealt with many of the typical experiences and legacies with which the victims of this illness may have to contend. The lucky ones are those who do not drift into chronic illness, as some of these will have a positive prognosis and a chance of going on to fulfil something of their original potential or even match it.

In this discussion, I have suggested that by appreciating the nature of the false messages which may be reaching the individual's brain, we are better able to understand the delusional thinking that is at the core of the illness. Certainly, recovered sufferers of varying levels of intelligence make very sensible comments about their experiences and suggest, albeit apologetically, that their ideas (however odd they may have seemed to others at the time) were appropriate *in the circumstances*. One man, who has managed to hold down responsible employment during most of his adult life despite several acute breakdowns, remarked to me recently that the bombardment of stimuli during these 'is like a radio receiving half-a-dozen stations at once'. What a frightening and isolating experience this must be! Small wonder that we note again and again in sufferers the phenomenon of a clinging, dependent relationship with one other human being, usually the mother. This pathological relationship is a hallmark of an acute schizophrenic illness, and is a visible demonstration of a 'drowning' human being using another as a lifeline.

As we have seen, most of the 'positive' symptoms are bizarre experiences which usually respond promptly to specific drug treatment. By contrast, the 'negative' symptoms are not helped significantly by drugs nor by any other available treatment, so they can be far more pervasive. Where they persist indefinitely, the course of the illness seems to be a degenerative one. The next chapter will take a further look at this subject and consider what we actually know about schizophrenia and its potential for successful treatment.

3 · What Do We Know about Schizophrenia?

What, then, do we know about schizophrenia? Although there seems to be an infinite abundance of theory and speculation about the illness, we still know very little about the origins and pervasiveness of this condition.

To start at the beginning, schizophrenia is a psychosis. Mental illness can be divided into two main types; the psychoses and the neuroses. Generally, we are familiar with the term 'neurosis' and have a reasonable understanding of its meaning. Most of us have minor neurotic traits. These may be irrational fears about mice or spiders, or of heights, of using lifts, of being 'closed in' or of being part of a large crowd. Other neurotic traits we may recognize are a tendency to fuss too much about keeping the house tidy or about following a particular routine. Usually we can laugh at such idiosyncrasies in ourselves, in our loved ones or in our colleagues. It is only when these traits prevent us from functioning properly in our everyday life that they require treatment and are diagnosed as neurosis. Importantly, the individual with a neurotic illness is only too aware of the problem, but this insight does not necessarily help relieve it. By contrast, in a psychotic illness individuals can lose touch with reality and be oblivious to the truth that they are ill. It is a sad irony that one of the main differences between these two types of illness is that those people who have a neurotic illness tend to seek a 'magic cure' with medication, although this rarely solves the problem, while individuals with a psychotic illness tend to reject the drugs which are often the only means by which their symptoms can be relieved.

Schizophrenia is the most common psychotic illness – the other main type is manic depressive illness, in which there can be dramatic variations in mood. There can be little doubt that there is some overlap between this condition and schizophrenia; they have several symptoms in common and it is not unknown for someone with a longstanding schizophrenic illness to exhibit all the signs of a manic depressive illness later in life, or vice versa. Indeed, some individuals are found to have some of the characteristics of each illness, and tend to be diagnosed as suffering from a 'schizo-affective disorder', while others who are less fortunate tend to elude both diagnosis and treatment. Recent work by Johnstone and her colleagues at Northwick Park Hospital[1] seems to support Crow's suggestion that these functional psychotic conditions may all be part of a continuum.[2]

Similarly, there is little understanding at present as to whether or not schizophrenia is a single entity. It certainly embraces a cluster of remarkably consistent symptoms, but the dramatic variations in the course and presentation of the illness suggest that there are several different sub-groups at least within the large population diagnosed as schizophrenic. Perhaps the following comment best sums up current thinking: 'Such differences have encouraged the view . . . that schizophrenia is in fact a group of related conditions. These conditions are assumed to have the same final common pathway of biochemical interactions, and lead to a similar series of consequences.'[3]

Theories about the causes of schizophrenia are plentiful and it sometimes seems that these are every bit as dependent on changing fashions as the clothes scene. They range from a genetic model, whereby sufferers inherit genes which make them predisposed to the illness, through to ideas that the condition is caused by families or by a sick society. As some of the strangest of these ideas have had a remarkable influence on current attitudes and our handling of schizophrenia, I plan to return to them later in this book.

In the meantime, what are the facts? We know of two factors that have a role in the development of this illness. The first is that brain damage can lead to a psychosis with all the features of a schizophrenic illness.[4] Indeed, long-term studies are now revealing that some people who develop schizophrenia have a history which points to obstetric complications at birth[5,6] that may be associated with brain damage, and they may turn out to form a very substantial sub-group of sufferers. The second factor is that the illness frequently runs in families. We know this because anyone with a blood relative with schizophrenia has a raised risk of contracting the illness. Although there is a risk of around 1 per cent for members of the general population, this increases to up to 50 per cent for the identical twin of a sufferer, and such twins do of course share exactly the same genes. The non-identical twin of a sufferer has a considerably reduced risk of 8 to 10 per cent – the same, in fact, as for other brothers and sisters of a sufferer. Similarly, an individual with parents who are both sufferers has around four times the chance of contracting the illness as someone with one schizophrenic parent (see Chapter 8, page 125). These risks apply whether or not members of the family grow up together or apart and clearly point to the likelihood of a strong genetic component in this condition. It is suspected that it is a disposition to develop schizophrenia that is inherited rather than the illness itself.

PRECIPITANTS

A schizophrenic illness can suddenly erupt or it can take a very long time to develop into a full-blown psychosis. Because several features crop up again and again prior to breakdown, it does seem that any of these may act as 'trigger factors', not to be confused with possible causes, that is, the origins of a schizophrenic illness. The four factors, any of which seem frequently to feature in the newly diagnosed sufferer's recent history are: (a) hormonal upheaval; (b) recovery from a virus; (c) move away from home and family; or (d) use of street drugs, such as LSD, amphetamines or cannabis. Let us take a look at each of these in turn.

(a) *Hormonal upheaval*: most first episodes of schizophrenia in women take place after puberty, childbirth, or, to a much lesser extent, the menopause. Most first episodes of the illness in men take place after puberty.

(b) *A virus*: it is not uncommon to find a newly diagnosed sufferer just getting over glandular fever or a bad attack of 'flu. Colin Blakemore comments in his book *The Mind Machine*: 'there have been many reports of schizophrenia . . . occurring shortly after attacks of viral encephalitis (sleeping sickness), measles, influenza and other virus infections.'[7] Similarly, there is evidence that the incidence of acute schizophrenic episodes increased with the great influenza epidemic of 1918.[8]

(c) *Away from home*: often families are unable to describe how their relative was immediately before a first breakdown because he or she was away from home at the time. This may well have made them more vulnerable.

(d) *Drug abuse*: it is becoming more common to find evidence of recent drug-taking, and particularly cannabis-smoking, before a first breakdown, and this may reflect a greater incidence of drug-taking among young people. Whatever the reason, some of them seem to be particularly vulnerable. In some cases, what seem to be the symptoms of a breakdown disappear after a few days without the offending drugs, so it is clear that the symptoms have been drug-induced. In others, the symptoms turn out to be the start of what is often a severe and persistent schizophrenic illness. Some sufferers believe that their illness started as a result of their drug-taking and wish that someone had warned them of the potential dangers.

INCIDENCE

It is not generally realized that while schizophrenia is one of the most serious illnesses known to mankind, it is also a common one. Indeed, it is estimated that there are at least one quarter of a million (diagnosed) sufferers in the United Kingdom alone. It is known that around one in every 100 of us will have such an illness at some time in our lives and that this is a reasonably constant figure throughout the world. However, there are a few conspicuous exceptions to this rule, and Fuller Torrey, a leading psychiatrist in the United States, has pointed out that 'in parts of Scandinavia the incidence is at least twice as common and in parts of western Ireland as many as one out of every twenty-five people is affected.'[9]

At the present time, the significance of this is not clear. Neither is it clear why there is a high incidence of Afro-Caribbeans being diagnosed as schizophrenic in Britain today. For example, a recent study found that second-generation immigrants from the Caribbean living in Nottingham are up to ten times more likely than white members of the population in the same area to be so diagnosed. This research team expected to find two cases among the 3,500 people of Caribbean origin aged between sixteen and forty-five years living in Nottingham, but found a total of twenty-seven.[10] This sort of finding has aroused anger and concern from critics, one of whom suggests that 'this diagnostic label, when used in many black patients, is nothing more than an attempt at translating some form of social distress or disturbance into clinical pathology'.[11]

Whatever the meaning of this raised risk in some populations and in some parts of the world, the saddest thing about the illness is that the majority of all first cases are diagnosed in young people between the ages of sixteen and twenty-five years (with the average age for females tending to be slightly older than for males).

SEASONAL BIRTHS

One other interesting statistic indicates that the timing of the conception of the baby may be as vital as the birth itself. A significantly raised proportion of births of individuals who become schizophrenic take place during the winter months, between December and April.

COURSE OF THE ILLNESS

It is clearly not possible to predict with confidence the course of a schizophrenic illness in any one individual. However, factors such as the incidence of schizophrenia in the individual's family and the degree of its severity can serve as pointers, as can the presence of certain features of the illness, such as serious *blunting of affect* (see page 38). It is often claimed that features such as a slow, insidious development of the illness, or having a withdrawn, introverted personality previously can be indicators of a poor prognosis. However, factors such as these can be successfully 'fudged' by the long delays that so often take place before diagnosis. It is certainly true that those cases which develop suddenly, erupting into bizarre behaviour overnight, tend to have a good prognosis. It is my belief that this may well be due to the fact that they have to receive prompt attention and treatment, thus avoiding damage which may be caused by the more usual delays.

We looked earlier at the two very different sorts of symptom found in this illness, the so-called 'positive' and 'negative' symptoms, and noted that the former are associated with an acute attack of schizophrenia and that the latter tend to represent the chronic form of the illness. We noted too that this is really an over-simplification as some of the 'negative' symptoms such as *lethargy* and *poverty of speech* can be part of an acute illness as well. Similarly, individuals with the chronic form of the illness can experience some of the 'positive' symptoms at times, and particularly during an acute breakdown. The picture can become even more blurred as some authorities refer to sufferers who have recurrent acute breakdowns as having a chronic illness, even though there may be no negative symptoms at all.

Perhaps it is less confusing if we refer to Crow's Type I and Type II syndromes.[12] The Type I syndrome covers the 'positive' symptoms which respond well to medication with, as Crow suggests, an expectation for the patient to suffer no intellectual impairment and for any damage to be reversible. The Type II syndrome represents the 'negative' symptoms, with a poor response to medication, possible intellectual impairment and a seemingly irreversible condition. Crow believes that the pathology in the Type I syndrome is a malfunctioning of the brain which may be connected with an over-abundance of dopamine in the brain cells (discussed later in this chapter), which can usually be remedied by drug treatment. By contrast, in the second syndrome there seem to be cell loss and actual structural changes in the brain. Although this might suggest that the two are unrelated conditions, this does not seem to be the case as it is not uncommon for both types of symptom to be observed in any one patient at any one time. Moreover, as Crow points out, some individuals can be seen to slip into the Type II syndrome after a second or third acute breakdown.

This factor, so often overlooked by those involved with the handling of this illness, has to be vitally important in preventive terms as it implies that *each and every breakdown brings with it a danger of irreversible damage*.

Initially, then, a diagnosis of schizophrenia gives little indication of the potential damage or risk to any one individual. We can only speak in general terms; some authorities use the 'rule of three', which divides sufferers into three groups, with one-third recovering almost completely, one-third remaining partially handicapped and vulnerable to intermittent relapses, and one-third damaged to the point that there can be no resumption of a normal lifestyle. Perhaps it is more meaningful to stay with the statistics that suggest that around 25 per cent of sufferers have no more than one breakdown and that at the other end of the continuum around 10 per cent become so damaged that they need hospitalization or similar institutional care for the rest of their lives. Between these two extremes, much depends on whether or not the individual develops the Type II syndrome. One mercifully small group of sufferers that we have not yet discussed are those who exhibit some or all of the 'positive' symptoms, being tormented by continuous 'voices' or delusions, but who obtain no relief from the available drugs. Carol North, now practising psychiatry, was one such patient, and she has vividly described her ordeal which lasted for many years.[13] She eventually recovered, but many others are not so fortunate, and we are still awaiting a treatment that will alleviate in some way the suffering for this particular group of the minority of sufferers who continue to need constant care.

Finally, we do know that this illness is frequently more severe in males than in females, and it has also been observed that the course of schizophrenia is more benign in some of the developing countries than in the more affluent industrialized societies.[14]

A FEW POSITIVE FEATURES

It has been realized for centuries that madness seems to be closely related to genius, and there can be no doubt at all that many sufferers have quite remarkable creative talents. Anyone who works with schizophrenia, and with the seemingly related manic depressive disorders, will be reminded daily of this phenomenon. Amongst this largely unknown population are gifted poets, artists and musicians. Many is the time I have heard a tinny old piano produce magical sounds in the hands of individuals whose lives have been blighted by this illness. Interestingly, one researcher has found the incidence of psychosis to be considerably higher in the near relatives of a large group of distinguished writers, poets and scholars than in the general population.[15] Crow has recently summed up the link between illnesses such as schizophrenia and manic depression and quite exceptional achievement thus:

Maybe the psychosis gene is very important for being human, that is, directly related to some of the things which we regard as the most important human achievements. It seems to me that when we have found it, then we will understand a great deal more about what it means to be human.[16]

A less well-recorded phenomenon, to which I have drawn attention elsewhere,[17] is the disproportionate number of sufferers who have been exceptionally talented in various forms of athletic activities and sports before their illness, suggesting that their eye and body coordination may have been well above average prior to this.

It has been noted that some schizophrenia sufferers (probably a distinct sub-group) seem to be unusually free of viral infections, and one piece of research indicated that the blood relatives of individuals who have a schizophrenic illness may be less vulnerable to viruses than the rest of the population.[18] There is also evidence that people with schizophrenia seem to be less vulnerable than the general population to suffering with rheumatoid arthritis.[19] As we noticed in Chapter 2, some are also remarkably oblivious to extremes of temperature and to pain. This can be dangerous as they tend not to notice discomfort which can be nature's warning sign that something is wrong.

Finally, one distinct physical advantage for a sizeable number of sufferers is a more than fair share of good looks, with a youthfulness of skin and features that completely belies their chronological age. This is a very real asset which can last throughout a lifetime, and one which many of the rest of us might well envy!

THE SUFFERING

Having looked briefly at one or two positive features of this type of illness that may well make the world a richer place, for the rest of us anyway, there can be no doubt at all that the cost to individual sufferers is appallingly high.

There is little agreement on the exact incidence of suicide in this illness. One piece of research suggested that about 10 per cent of all schizophrenics kill themselves,[20] and another found that three of thirty-nine first-admission cases committed suicide during a fifteen-year follow-up period.[21] One researcher looked a little more closely at those who seemed to be at risk by comparing thirty sufferers who had committed suicide with thirty who had not, and he found that suicide was more common in younger men, if the condition took a remitting course and if a depressed mood had been a prominent part of the clinical picture.[22] One of the difficulties in establishing a more definite figure for this deadly toll is that some coroners have shown a pronounced reluctance to record a verdict of suicide on many of the self-inflicted violent deaths in schizophrenia. For example, a psychiatrist recently reported that one of his schizophrenic patients jumped from a high building and her death was recorded as 'misadventure'.[23] Another difficulty is that the delay in the diagnosis of this condition means that many unexplained suicides in students and other young people in the optimum risk age group may well be attributable to the nightmare of a developing and undiagnosed schizophrenic illness.[24]

That schizophrenia has a crippling effect on the lifestyle of many sufferers is demonstrated by the fact that less than half of the men with the illness get married. Although more women do, their divorce and separation rates are very much higher than those for the average population. As we shall see in Chapter 10, even those who are well enough to resume a normal lifestyle find it difficult to do so because of a diagnosis which can bar the way to pensionable jobs, affordable insurance, a driving licence, fostering or adoption and emigration, as well as creating many other obstacles. The extent of the stigma and discrimination is such that schizophrenia might well be described as the final taboo. Tragically, the ignorance and attitudes that have led to this sort of stigma militate successfully against early diagnosis of a treatable disease.

Let us take a closer look now at the sort of treatment that is available for schizophrenia.

TREATMENT

Until the discovery of the neuroleptic drugs in the 1950s (see page 52), the vast majority of all those who developed a schizophrenic illness were destined to spend the rest of their tormented lives in hospital. At the turn of the century, the medical profession had no tools with which to alleviate the miseries of the insane and tried out a truly amazing assortment of so-called treatments, including blood-letting and purges of various kinds. Strait-jackets and padded cells were used when patients became violent, and there was seemingly little emphasis on caring and nurturing. However, there can be no doubt that just containing and restraining the victims of an unrelieved psychotic nightmare presented a mammoth task in itself. The wretched misery of life in the old mental hospitals up until the middle of this century is well documented.

During the 1920s it was noted that some schizophrenic patients seemed to gain a measure of relief from their symptoms on coming out of a hypoglycaemic coma, and this led to the common practice of injecting patients with doses of insulin until their blood sugar level dropped to the point of unconsciousness. They were later brought round with a glucose drip, and a series of such treatments would be continued over several months. Some doctors believed this provided a sedative effect and also a beneficial influence on patients' appetite. This was a very labour-intensive operation and by the time insulin coma treatment was abandoned, there was little remaining enthusiasm for this approach.

In the mid-1930s psycho-surgery became popular and in particular the prefrontal lobotomy, involving the destruction of the nerve fibres on each side of the brain. Whereas this barbaric-sounding approach may have helped a few individuals suffering from an agitated depression resistant to other measures, it was never shown to have any beneficial effect on the symptoms of schizophrenia. Despite this, many such operations were performed on individuals with this illness, and they may well have been further and irretrievably damaged by surgery that was known to cause personality change in some patients.

Shortly after the start of psycho-surgery, the passing of an electric current through the brain was found to be helpful in relieving depression in some individuals. Electroconvulsive therapy was never found to be of specific benefit to schizophrenic patients, except perhaps where a severe depression was the dominating feature of their illness. However, this did not stop this measure being used regularly in the treatment of schizophrenia for many years.

Perhaps it was inevitable, in view of the ineffectiveness of the treatments that were available to the medical profession, that a different approach to schizophrenia should be greeted with growing enthusiasm. In particular, the practice of 'talking therapies' was increasing in popularity, with psychoanalysts claiming that they could treat this illness, which they believed to be the result of faulty upbringing and early, forgotten childhood traumas. Maybe it is not surprising that their contribution added little to the relief of the misery of schizophrenia, and it is interesting to note that Sigmund Freud, the father of psychoanalysis, had warned that psychosis would one day be found to be of physical origin. He himself eventually declined to work with this type of illness.

THE NEUROLEPTIC DRUGS

All things considered, then, the outlook for people contracting this disease was no happier than it had been for many decades by the early 1950s when a French naval surgeon called Laboret was searching for something to prevent post-operative shock. He tried a new drug called chlorpromazine and was impressed with the relaxing effect this had on his patients, without affecting their alertness. He wondered if this drug could be useful in psychiatry. It quickly became evident that the drug was indeed useful in this field and that it had a specific action on patients with the florid symptoms of an acute schizophrenic illness. By 1953 the drug was in regular use and minor miracles were seen to be happening every day. Very soon, more drugs of the same kind were available, and so great was the impact of this type of medication on schizophrenia that nurses who were working at that time still talk of long-term severely ill patients – some of them potentially very dangerous – becoming calm, approachable and, eventually, well enough to enjoy a reasonable quality of life.

What, then, was happening with these drugs? It was not until the 1960s that scientists began to understand why they might be an antidote to this type of psychosis. The typical side-effects produced by the drugs led to suspicion about dopamine, one of the substances that act as cell messengers in our brains. Parkinson's disease is connected with levels of dopamine that are too low and it was soon clear that some schizophrenic patients treated with these drugs initially developed Parkinsonian-type symptoms. It seemed possible, therefore, that chlorpromazine and other drugs of the same kind were dopamine antagonists, that is, they reduced the level of dopamine in the brain. Two other discoveries tended to support this theory. First, the drug L-Dopa which increases the release of dopamine from nerve-endings and so alleviates Parkinson's disease, has also been found to precipitate symptoms like those experienced in a schizophrenic illness. Second, amphetamines, when given in high doses, raise the dopamine levels in the brain and are known to produce schizophrenic-like symptoms. It seemed, therefore, that the neuroleptic drugs were acting as an antidote to the florid symptoms of schizophrenia because they checked an over-abundance of dopamine in the brain cells.

These were heady days; not only had a miracle antidote been found for the bizarre symptoms of the acute form of schizophrenia, but it seemed that the cause of the illness was about to be revealed. However, although the 'dopamine theory' has continued to be the dominating one to this day, it has in fact revealed frustratingly little about the origins of schizophrenia. Important questions remain unanswered. For example, it is very noticeable that any Parkinsonian side-effects usually appear within twenty-four hours of starting the drugs, but that real relief from the symptoms of an acute breakdown does not take place for another two to three weeks. It may well be that the effect of the drugs on the available dopamine supply will turn out to be less significant than some other, more delayed action. For example, it is interesting that chlorpromazine is a recognized appetite stimulant and is used for severe cases of persistent hiccups, acute vomiting and cases of diarrhoea. If it has such a vital part to play in such conditions, then it is not impossible that the gut plays a significant role in a schizophrenic illness, and this is discussed in more detail in Chapter 8.

Meanwhile, there is no doubt at all that chlorpromazine and various other similar drugs have transformed the face of schizophrenia. Quite simply, they are the only tool we have at the present time with which we can effectively arrest an acute schizophrenic breakdown. They are known as 'neuroleptic drugs', 'antipsychotic' drugs or 'major tranquillizers'. The latter name has led to misunderstandings about this valuable medication at a time when the widespread prescribing of minor tranquillizers has deservedly fallen into disrepute. To my mind, the expression 'major tranquillizer' is a misnomer for drugs that are in no way a 'heavier' version of the 'minor tranquillizers' and that, most importantly, *do not share their addictive characteristics*. Any sedative effect is achieved as the direct result of blocking of dopamine receptors, thus relieving the sort of torment discussed in the last chapter. This in turn has the effect of actually freeing and revitalizing patients, enabling them to begin to function effectively again.

There are several groups of neuroleptic drugs now in everyday use, but although there has been considerable research since the discovery of the specific effect of chlorpromazine on an acute schizophrenic illness, most of the available drugs are really variations on a single theme. They all block the dopamine receptors, and to a greater or lesser extent they have a similar curbing effect on certain other brain cell messengers, or neurotransmitters as they are called. Some have a more sedating effect than others and some tend to give rise to more side-effects. There can be considerable variation in the way individuals respond to one or the other drug, and it may take some little time before sufferers are satisfactorily stabilized on the right one for them. Most of the drugs are available in tablet form or can be administered as a *depot injection*, that is, an injection given intramuscularly, preferably in the buttocks, and which is released gradually into the system from an oily base. Injections give long-term protection, for periods of two to four weeks, and there is reason to believe that the drug is better absorbed by this method. Another advantage is that they provide an opportunity for health professionals to monitor the sufferer's medication and to follow up those who fail to turn up for their next injection. Nevertheless, some doctors hesitate to prescribe injections unless and until the illness becomes well and truly 'established'. Similarly, some sufferers opt to take their medication orally and can keep well doing this. A frequent problem here is that people with schizophrenia are notoriously forgetful, even reluctant, about taking a regular dose of tablets, making the risk of a sudden relapse more real.

Just how effective are the neuroleptic drugs? They have proved to be beneficial in two ways: they frequently and promptly relieve the symptoms of an acute schizophrenic breakdown (and we have no other means of achieving this) and they also play an important part in preventing further breakdowns. Research consistently points to an overwhelming incidence of relapse within two years for those individuals who do not continue to take the drugs. The author of an overview of twenty-four studies observed that 65 per cent who received placebos relapsed, in contrast to 30 per cent of those who were maintained on neuroleptic drugs.[25] Although this is an impressive result, it is clear that the drugs do not protect all sufferers from relapse – and other important factors are discussed later in the chapter – but that most have a better chance of staying well if they persevere with them. As MIND, the active pressure group for the mentally ill, is not noted for its enthusiasm for a medical model of mental illness, comments on the front page of its special report on this type of medication are all the more interesting:

Major tranquillizers are the single most important and effective treatment for serious mental disorders such as schizophrenia. . . . Many people with serious mental disorders are able to lead a worthwhile life in the community thanks to major tranquillizers. . . . All treatments have advantages and disadvantages. For many people with serious mental disorders, any problems caused by the side-effects of major tranquillizers are outweighed by the good they do.[26]

SIDE-EFFECTS

We have discussed some of the advantages of these drugs; what, then, are the disadvantages? As we know, all medication can cause unpleasant side-effects in some individuals; sadly, the neuroleptic drugs are no exception. In the main, these drugs provoke Parkinsonian-type symptoms, seemingly due to their dopamine-restricting function. These extra-pyramidal symptoms may include tremors and a feeling of restlessness which makes the individual feel compelled to be constantly on the move. There may be facial, hand or leg movements, or twisting of the head, neck and body. At worst, there may be an acute reaction of 'lock-jaw', with stiffening of the muscles or rolling back of the eyes. These side-effects, while potentially very unpleasant, are usually of a temporary nature only, with an immediate response to anti-Parkinsonian drugs. It used to be common practice to prescribe such drugs automatically with the neuroleptic medication, but this is no longer the case. Ideally, patients are warned of the possibility of such side-effects and monitored carefully for their appearance so that any appropriate action can be taken immediately. Where the side-effects tend to persist, then the antidote medication is prescribed as an ongoing measure. Other side-effects can include reduced blood pressure, unwanted weight gain, and in some cases feelings of apathy and drowsiness, although the latter are more usually symptoms of the illness itself.

TARDIVE DYSKINESIA

Unhappily, there is one serious complication which may be associated with the long-term usage of these drugs, especially in the elderly. Tardive dyskinesia is a distressing condition which manifests itself in some individuals particularly when the neuroleptic drugs are withdrawn, causing involuntary movements mainly of the face and tongue. These sufferers may be resistant to treatment except for, ironically, the administration of increased amounts of the neuroleptic medication. Irrelevant use of the anti-Parkinsonian drugs may be implicated in the development of this condition, and this is one reason why they should not be prescribed unless a need for them is indicated. Little as yet is understood about tardive dyskinesia, and some elderly people with schizophrenia, *who have never been on neuroleptic medication*, develop it. In fact, the condition was known to exist before the advent of these drugs and some research suggests it may be associated with the sort of brain damage seemingly connected with the Type II syndrome (see page 47).[27,28] Nevertheless, we do not yet have sufficient knowledge to understand the role of the drugs in the development of this condition. Sadly, we seem to have no choice but to abandon sufferers to the horrors and dangers of unrelieved psychosis, as in the days before the drugs were discovered, or encourage them to take drugs that may hold out such long-term risks for a minority of individuals. On the whole, most people with schizophrenia do choose, sooner or later, to 'live for today', to fight an existing enemy rather than worry too much about a possible future one. For example, one sufferer, a lecturer in humanities, comments:

If I cease to take my medication, I become delusional again in about three weeks, but if I take my medication I have a good chance of remaining sane. With the help of medication and as long as my circumstances remain as favourable as they are now, I can live a slightly handicapped but overall useful and worthwhile life.[29]

This raises important considerations which are frequently forgotten by those who prescribe ongoing neuroleptic medication for sufferers in the community. While the medication may be 'magic' for many individuals who would never have been able to move out of hospital before its discovery, its effects are severely limited if certain other factors are not taken into account. The sufferer quoted above implies that staying on the drugs *and continuing favourable circumstances* are the two main components of staying well as far as he is concerned. Too often it is overlooked that good health in the community will also be dependent upon the achieving of a rewarding lifestyle (however modest this might have to be if the residual handicap is very real). It is unrealistic to expect people with schizophrenia to remain well without recourse to a lifestyle that provides adequate stimulation and protection from unreasonable stress. It is irresponsible to expect them to remain well without continuous and vigilant monitoring of their medication. In most cases, this will need adjustment from time to time, and for some it may include the use of other complementary drugs such as carbamazepine or Lithium (the main treatment for manic depression) if mood levels become a problem, or perhaps an anti-depressant.

TOWARDS AN OPEN DOOR POLICY

The dramatic effect of the neuroleptic drugs on schizophrenia led to equally dramatic changes in the mental hospitals by the end of the 1950s. Gone were the days when most of the wards needed to be locked, both for the safety of the patients and for the safety of others. With the opening of most of the hospital wards came an opening of the hospital doors too. One of the most positive features of the Mental Health Act 1959 was its emphasis on the concept of *voluntary admission* to mental hospitals, and the vast majority of individuals needing in-hospital treatment since that time have been admitted as voluntary patients who cannot be detained against their will. Perhaps more importantly, while the resources were still available, many of these sufferers were able to gain admission to hospital at their own request, rather than just when others were suggesting that this was desirable. This legislation embodied all the optimism of the latter years of the 1950s when it was believed that the neuroleptic drugs together with the new 'open door' policy would do away with the need for the long-term containment of the mentally ill. Before very long, there was talk of 'community care' and the closing down of the big old hospitals. People with schizophrenia should be able to stay out in the community and to live rewarding lives. This was indeed a time of hope.

4 · Denial

Well, what happened to the hopes of the 1950s, when the introduction of the neuroleptic drugs (see page 52) and the new 'open door' policy seemed set to change the face of schizophrenia? A leading American psychiatrist commented during the 1980s that 'except for the advent of the [neuroleptic] drugs, it is very doubtful whether persons with schizophrenia are any better off in the United States today than they were thirty years ago'.[1] Could such a claim be made about the fate of sufferers in other countries? What happens now, for example, to relatives or friends seeking help when they see that something is very wrong with someone dear and familiar to them?

FIRST RESPONSES

As most of us do at times of stress, parents usually turn first to family and close friends when they become anxious about a son or daughter. However, most people do not know much about mental illness, and even less about schizophrenia, so this usually achieves little. All but those really close to the individual will probably notice nothing anyway for some considerable time, and anxious parents will listen to platitudes about the 'generation gap' or the young person's need to draw away and become independent.

PROFESSIONAL RESPONSES

More seriously, it is not at all uncommon for these same anxious parents to receive similar responses from professionals when they later turn to them for help. Back in the 1960s, two North American psychiatrists warned that the sort of change that involved a normal outgoing adolescent becoming shy, reclusive, lonely and irritable, *without an obvious change in environment or signs of physical disease*, could be indicative of a developing schizophrenic illness, and that families should seek help in these circumstances.[2] Many do just that only to find themselves listening to more platitudes about teenagers needing space for growing up. Too many experts, it seems, choose to focus on the family's anxiety and interpret this in such a way that this provides an explanation for the sick individual's altered behaviour. Instead of *hearing and listening to* what is being said, they thus turn away from a young person in deep distress. Significantly, a study carried out at Northwick Park Hospital in 1985, involving 462 new cases of schizophrenia, confirms that this is a common experience. The researchers examined the results of families' efforts to obtain assessment and treatment for their relatives. They found that even where sick individuals were exhibiting extremely bizarre and, in some cases, clearly dangerous behaviour, delays in obtaining help often lasted over a year. In 10 per cent of all cases, at least nine prior contacts were made with at least one service before help was provided. These workers concluded that their findings 'must cause serious disquiet to psychiatrists and others responsible for the services'.[3]

AVOIDANCE AND DENIAL

Families and friends frequently ask, after such frustrating and dangerous delays as these, 'What could we have said that would have made them realize he was ill?' *What indeed?* Unless there is a willingness in the listener to hear what is being said, it makes little difference what words we use. Although this is not expressed explicitly, the message from the experts is really 'Let's wait and see'. *But why?* Is it possible that any thinking person would suppose it helpful to leave someone probably developing a schizophrenic illness to flounder around in a lonely nightmare for longer than is absolutely necessary? What of the havoc that delay can wreak on his or her personal relationships, not to mention hopes and plans for the future? More importantly, is this sort of delay defensible on *health grounds*? Is there, for example, any other treatable and potentially serious illness for which we have a policy of 'Let's wait and see'? Judy Weleminsky, when Director of the National Schizophrenia Fellowship, commented:

General ignorance among the population and a prevalence of mis-conceptions, combined with resistance on the part of professionals to diagnose, results in catastrophically late diagnosis. I am not aware of any other disease in which it is thought beneficial to delay and avoid diagnosis. Why is it true for schizophrenia?[4]

Although no one can begin to answer that question adequately, the tragedy of avoidable suffering and wastage of potential continues. It has been known for a long time that a second or third schizophrenic breakdown can lead into the chronic form of the illness with, as we have noted, irreversible damage. In fact, unrelieved schizophrenic symptoms are indeed bad news. It is not surprising, therefore, that we find two examples of recent work suggesting that early intervention makes sense. In a government-sponsored community project at Buckingham, GPs followed up *first cries for help* from concerned families and, if appropriate, they referred the individual for assessment to a specialist team. If the first tentative diagnosis was confirmed by these professionals, then low doses of neuro-leptic medication were prescribed immediately, together with an educational and supportive programme for sufferer and family, so that they could appreciate what was happening and find ways of coping with the individual's vulnerability. These workers claim that they received far more referrals than would usually be expected from GPs, and that this preventive work appeared to arrest the disease process at an early stage.[5] Similarly, researchers at North-wick Park Hospital found the length of the period of delay between onset of symptoms and admission to hospital to be a significant factor in predicting poor outcome in a schizophrenic illness. They suggest that this may well mean that the persistence of symptoms untreated by neuroleptic drugs may lead to abnormality which cannot be completely reversed by subsequent treatment.[6] In fact, we have no reason to believe that schizophrenia is different to any other potentially treatable illness; the sooner the intervention, the better.

CONSPIRACY OF SILENCE?

Even when a diagnosis of schizophrenia is eventually made, it is quite uncommon for this to be shared with patient or family at that time. All too often, patients are discharged after a first breakdown without any idea of what has happened to them or what this could mean for their future. Gwynneth Hemmings, General Director of the Schizophrenia Association of Great Britain, has pointed out that 'the schizophrenic patient is left in a terrifying vacuum . . . deprived of the all essential information about his disease',[7] and many sufferers will confirm the truth of these words. So often they have learned to cope with their symptoms only when they were eventually given an explanation for them. Is this surprising if we remember the sort of distorted messages that are part of the nightmare of a schizophrenic breakdown? How on earth can sufferers be expected to deal with vivid memories of this nightmare without an explanation for what has happened to them? Perhaps more importantly, how can they pick up the remains of valued relationships and deal with the future without an explanation for any residual symptoms, or even an acknowledgment that there are any symptoms at all?

When psychiatrists are asked, 'Why this conspiracy of silence?', they are likely to explain that between one-quarter and one-third of all those who experience a schizophrenic breakdown will recover spontaneously, with no further relapse. For example, Bleuler's finding in 1978 that 'at least 25 per cent of all schizophrenics recover entirely [after one breakdown] and remain recovered for good'[8] is frequently quoted. The argument goes that these fortunate individuals can be spared a premature diagnosis that has so much stigma attached to it. However, this does not take account of the fact that Bleuler's criteria for 'recovery' allow for the *persistence of delusions and perceptual disturbance*. Bearing in mind the effects of these sorts of distorted messages and ideas on individuals who have been denied any explanation for them, it seems highly unlikely that this so-called fortunate group of sufferers will achieve much quality of life under these circumstances. *And what about the other 75 per cent who are at risk of further breakdown* and particularly so if they are given no diagnosis or information with which to protect themselves? Although we know that each breakdown brings with it a risk of irreversible and tragic damage,[9] some psychiatrists actually *await at least one relapse* in the patient before being prepared to acknowledge the diagnosis. The cost of such an approach would seem to be unpardonably high and it would seem reasonable that the withholding of a diagnosis in such cases may one day be regarded as negligence. Importantly, there are difficulties with determining a diagnosis of schizophrenia, and some of these are discussed in some detail in Chapter 8 of this book. The issue under discussion is not the ability to make a firm diagnosis; rather, it is the decision to withhold such a diagnosis from those most concerned or to withhold the sharing of vital information that could and should be made available even while the diagnosis remains tentative only.

So sufferers often remain in ignorance throughout a first stay in hospital. The delusional content of a schizophrenic illness makes this situation something of a black comedy; many 'recover' without understanding they have had an illness of any kind. More often than not, they do not learn anything from hospital staff which would help to change their minds, let alone understand their experiences. This is not a characteristic of British hospitals only; a sufferer in the United States has protested that the staff left him to his own devices: 'After about three weeks, I started feeling better, thanks to the medication. Still the staff left me alone. Didn't they know what was behind my illness?'[10] This man has since obtained the information he needs to survive and, as can be seen from his comment, he understands the role of the drugs he takes. What about less fortunate individuals like Ray, whom I met recently?

Ray is a bright, good-looking young man who had enough insight left at the time of his first breakdown to seek help and to agree to go into hospital. On arriving there, he became scared and started to run away. He was brought back and later given an injection against his will, and eighteen months later he described with a shudder the memory of being held down by several members of staff. Despite the potential insight he had shown earlier, no one in the hospital attempted to discuss with him what was happening and the purpose of the medication, either at that time *or later*. Sadly, this omission was compounded by the fact that Ray was one of those unlucky patients who initially have almost immediate side-effects, and his were severe and frightening. There was some delay before these were dealt with, and by that time Ray had developed a seething hatred for the doctor who prescribed the injection. Since leaving hospital, he has refused even to discuss continuing with his injections and does not keep his out-patient appointments. Ironically, his is the type of schizophrenic illness that responds really well to the neuroleptic drugs, and to look at Ray no one would suspect that there was anything wrong with him. However, due to his continuing ignorance about his own condition, and to his unfortunate memories of hospital, he takes only a minimum of the oral medication prescribed for him (even he has to acknowledge that he is not really able to function at all without this). This is not enough to allow this bright young man to fulfil his potential and live a normal lifestyle. He is tormented by paranoid ideas and his resulting inability to make rewarding relationships. Life in the family home is tense and difficult; his two brothers find they cannot cope with his unpredictable behaviour, so they avoid him when they can. His career seems to be ever more precarious because of his preoccupation with his delusional ideas and his frequent absences from work. On meeting with Ray, I was acutely aware of the depth of his suffering and impressed by his courage in trying to deal with it. He has tried to rationalize what is happening to him and has decided he is being punished for past 'evils', and that being 'conned' into hospital was part of this. He sets himself limits to the length of the sentence he must serve and says wistfully that it will be all right after Christmas (or Easter, or whenever). Sadly, each potential milestone comes and goes . . .

It is rare, then, to find sufferers who have had the chance to learn or to talk about schizophrenia in hospital. Even those who are used to discussing their symptoms in the community tend to take it for granted that these are not a topic for discussion back in hospital. A third year nursing student visiting a meeting of her local National Schizophrenia Fellowship group one evening marvelled at the way several sufferers had been able to verbalize their experiences so clearly. She explained to them that she felt very inadequate because she had been given to understand that it was a waste of time to try to talk with withdrawn schizophrenic patients on the ward. Such comments are frequently heard up and down the country. This does mean that potential skill and therapy are withheld at a time when sufferers particularly need constant reassurance and repeated opportunities to test and re-test reality. It also means that, in so far as schizophrenic patients are concerned, scarce hospital beds tend to be used just for the monitoring and adjusting of medication. This has to be a waste of precious human resources.

So much for the patient being kept in ignorance, but what of the carers? How do they fare in their efforts to be supportive to the sufferer? An article in *The Bulletin of The Royal College of Psychiatrists* comments that the frequent problem mentioned by relatives is the difficulty in obtaining factual and practical advice. The article concludes:

Although most relatives, like most sufferers, do eventually become aware of the diagnosis, it is rare for them to be given this information as part of a long-term plan of management which they are invited to share with professional staff and patient, and even more unusual for them to be told early in the course of the disorder.[11]

Consider one leading authority's comment on the tightrope that families and friends walk when trying to support a chronically ill or recovering schizophrenic sufferer in the community:

On the one hand, too much social stimulation, experienced by the patient as social intrusiveness, may lead to an acute relapse. On the other hand, too little stimulation will exacerbate any tendency already present towards social withdrawal, slowness, underactivity and an apparent lack of motivation.[12]

Clearly, considerable skills are required if the right sort of balance is going to be achieved! Such skills can only be based on a real understanding of the experiences and special needs of people with this illness. Too often, families are deprived of the opportunity to acquire such skills. Too often, those closest to the sufferer are left in ignorance, floundering in an unhappy nightmare in which they have no control over what is happening to them. Most of us cope with the uncertainties of life by creating some sort of order for ourselves. We seek practical ways of resolving any problems that come along and feel secure when we succeed in this. Where there is little understanding of what is happening, families are deprived of these normal coping mechanisms. This helps no one at all, and puts the mental health of the whole household at risk. *It certainly serves no useful purpose at all for the sufferer.* If families are well informed about this illness, they learn that an accepting environment is all-important for their schizophrenic relative, with emphasis on building up an inevitably shattered self-esteem. Within such a climate, it is possible to keep their aims for the sufferer realistic, but nevertheless to provide enough stimulation to avoid the dangers of 'social withdrawal' as outlined above. If families know about and understand the symptoms of the illness, then they are more likely to cope with their relative's delusional thinking and hallucinations, so helping him or her to keep a grasp of reality. Above all, they will understand and know the importance of encouraging the sufferer to persist with taking the prescribed medication. All of these aims might seem to be ambitious, but they are paramount if the family is to survive. It is difficult to imagine how they can be achieved properly without the sort of vital information about the illness that is so often withheld. Small wonder that Wing comments: 'It is extraordinary that so many relatives do manage to find a way of living with schizophrenia that provides the patient with a supportive and non-threatening home.'[13]

CONFIDENTIALITY

A recent publication, *Mental Hospital Closures*, suggests that psychiatrists need to spend as much time with the relatives as with the patients and that 'this will require a complete change of approach on the behalf of many psychiatrists who tend to regard patient confidentiality as sacrosanct'.[14]

Let us examine this a little more closely. Even when a diagnosis of schizophrenia is acknowledged, some psychiatrists insist that they will not see close relatives unless the patient is present and agrees to this. By taking this line, they are ignoring the fact that a schizophrenic illness can make the sufferer lose touch with reality. By doing so, they choose to abandon their potentially psychotic patients to carers who have no recourse to their professional expertise and, in some cases, not even a lifeline in times of need.

These psychiatrists also deny themselves the benefit of learning about their patients' daily lifestyle and progress from the people who know them best. What a price to pay for medical 'confidentiality'! As we have already seen, many schizophrenic patients suffer from paranoid symptoms which are typically associated with those closest and dearest to them, and these doctors collude with any such delusional ideas by shutting the carers out of the picture. They leave themselves open to being deceived by patients who may be desperately defending themselves from being recognized as relapsing. Psychotic patients are notoriously effective at protecting themselves in this way over a short period, such as in an interview situation. Choosing to work in a vacuum in this way can lead to inappropriate advice from the doctors concerned, such as encouraging a move from home at an inappropriate time or giving backing to a premature return to college. Finally, they exhibit a profound lack of knowledge about the reality of coping with a schizophrenic illness in the community.

CRISIS INTERVENTION

Too many carers report unbelievable traumas when they try to obtain help for sufferers at times of crisis. They find themselves facing seemingly insurmountable obstacles, and it might be useful to re-cap on some of these. As we have noted already, GPs may maintain that they cannot force their attentions on a patient who will not come to their surgery. Although many will request a domiciliary visit from a psychiatrist at such times, some seem to be unaware of this facility while others are reluctant to use it. Where this is not a problem, there may be resource problems, with delays of several days before the psychiatrist can make a home visit. Once medical professionals consider that a formal admission to hospital is necessary, they then contact the local Social Services department, seeking an assessment from an approved social worker (ASW) – that is, a social worker approved to work with the mental health legislation. All of this can take some considerable time, and ASWs may arrive only to find that sufferers have 'made a run for it', terrified by the comings and goings of the different professionals. Alternatively, sufferers' behaviour may well be 'normalized' by the threat of danger and the social workers may be deceived by this. Encouraged to find the 'least restrictive alternative' to hospital whenever possible, these professionals have the right to refuse to make the application for admission if they do not believe this to be essential. In these circumstances, the family should be informed by one of the professionals concerned *that the law allows for the 'nearest relative' to make the application*. Often this does not happen. The Northwick Park Hospital *Study of First Episodes of Schizophrenia* found that difficult situations could have been avoided if relatives had known about domiciliary visits for patients who refuse to visit doctors, and if they had known that the nearest relative could make application for the patient's admission to hospital.[15] It seems, therefore, that although necessary safeguards for potentially vulnerable sufferers have been built into the system, some key professionals are unaware of, or ignore, them. I have given a simple explanation of the workings of the law and a definition of 'the nearest relative' elsewhere.[16]

Thus the mental health legislation can sometimes be seen to obstruct rather than facilitate the admission to hospital of seriously ill patients, with those closest to them left to play out a potentially tragic drama *on their own*. In fact, they can find themselves deserted by mental health professionals in their time of need. The most graphic description of how this feels was summed up recently by the daughter of a frail and elderly mother who has had to live through this situation with a very sick son several times. 'She gets so frightened, she wets herself,' she told me. Maybe it is not surprising that a survey in the mid-1980s involving 889 families in the National Schizophrenia Fellowship has revealed that 161 sufferers obtained no help for their first schizophrenic episode until the police intervened.[17] Although theirs is a controversial role from the point of view of many advocates of civil rights, and although they are not trained to work with the mentally ill, the police do have powers under the Mental Health Act 1983. Families all over the country frequently pay tribute to their intervention. At the end of 1989, an NSF survey carried out on behalf of the Department of Health revealed that, among the 563 members who took part, the police are the most highly rated service when it comes to caring for the mentally ill.[18] It is not too hard to imagine the sort of distress and suffering that lies behind the findings of both these surveys!

DISCUSSION

Clearly, something is very wrong when it comes to the seeking and obtaining of help for individuals developing a schizophrenic illness. In my work, over many years, I constantly meet carers who greet me despairingly with 'You won't believe what has happened to us.' I do believe it; I'm almost word-perfect before they start, I have heard it so often. It is a disturbing story that few thinking individuals would credit unless they experienced it themselves. The fact that it can happen again and again seems quite incomprehensible and suggests that the nightmare world of psychosis is quite sane by comparison with our present approach to its treatment.

Those who contract a schizophrenic illness are all too often condemned to long months, sometimes years, of misery before help is forthcoming. Although we have no evidence at all to contradict the common-sense view that the course of this serious illness may be influenced by early intervention, professionals still turn and look the other way until such time as the individual's condition can no longer be ignored. While the torture continues unabated, cherished ambitions and plans for the future are threatened, often lost for ever, and valued relationships destroyed. While a son, daughter, wife or husband, brother or sister becomes unrecognizable and unreachable, families are amazed that no one will listen and understand that they are trying to describe an abnormality beyond their wildest dreams. When, eventually, the diagnosis is established, they and the sufferer may or may not be told of this. They will certainly be fortunate if they are given vital information on schizophrenia sooner rather than later, enabling the individual to cope better with residual symptoms and to avoid further breakdowns.

Even when a diagnosis of schizophrenia is at last acknowledged and brought out into the open, carers are frequently devastated to find that when they see the first signs of a threatened relapse and seek professional help, they come up against the unvoiced 'Let's wait and see' syndrome once more. Instead of being listened to, they are again subjected to platitudes that are meant to explain the reason for any perceived change in behaviour. Having battled their way through similar experiences prior to a relative's first break-down, families reporting the early danger signs of relapse often find themselves facing these same attitudes all over again. They may be told they are fussing too much or, more disturbingly, that the sufferer is being 'attention-seeking' or 'manipulative', with something like 'You see, he knows how to make you anxious, Mrs — '!

I have reported elsewhere[19] the trials of one mother trying to obtain help before her daughter relapsed. Jackie is now twenty-seven years of age and has suffered from auditory hallucinations almost continuously since her illness started in her late teens. Although nothing had relieved these particular symptoms, her mother and sister had managed to support Jackie in the community for two years. At the first signs of relapse, her mother immediately asked for help at the hospital Jackie attended twice weekly, but her pleas were ignored. One month later, when Jackie was admitted to the same hospital under an emergency section, her mother had still not been granted the courtesy of the interview she had requested with the psychiatrist. The last time I saw Jackie, she had been in hospital for twenty months. The professionals who had ignored her mother's warnings had not been able to do anything to undo the damage wreaked by this further breakdown. . . . Since this further tragedy for Jackie and those who love her, work carried out in Birmingham[20] has confirmed something that families trying to cope with this illness have known all along; they do recognize the first signs of relapse in their schizophrenic relatives before others do so, often at the vital stage when they still have enough insight to agree to accept preventive treatment.

Some professionals, while paying lip-service to a diagnosis of schizophrenia, then negate its meaning. For example, a mother was recently told by a senior nurse that her daughter was not ill; she would be perfectly all right if she took her medication regularly. This sort of double-talk is particularly dangerous when it is a rationalization for withdrawing care which is desperately needed. That was the case in this example and the nurse was referring to a young woman who has been schizophrenic for seven years and who has had particularly horrific and bizarre experiences during that time. Furthermore, she has not been helped to develop insight into her illness and her need for neuroleptic drugs.

So those closest to individuals with this illness find that their attempts to prevent a further crisis tend to be ignored. Perhaps it is even more startling to find that sufferers themselves can argue in vain that they are experiencing a return of their schizophrenic symptoms! In view of the delusionary nature of this illness, it is a cause for celebration when sufferers achieve enough insight into their own vulnerability to recognize the early signs of threatened relapse. Lee, now in his late twenties, had worked hard to reach this admirable state of affairs, but was let down on three counts by professionals who could dramatically affect his well-being. He was so ill by the time that he was finally diagnosed that Lee was convinced that the rest of the world was mad and he was the only sane person left; a belief that alienated him from everyone, including his caring family. It took a long time – twenty months, in fact – before he was well enough to take up part-time sheltered employment, and another eighteen months before he could take up his old semi-skilled work. This gradual recovery was achieved after many false starts as it took a long time to find the right neuroleptic medication for him and even longer for it to have any real effect on his symptoms. From that point on, Lee started to recover some of his old self-esteem and, later, his powers of concentration. He was given a great deal of support and he gradually began to believe that he could live a normal life again.

Many months later, and not long after he eventually returned to full-time employment, his GP and a community psychiatric nurse, who seemed to have no real idea of the extent of his previous incapacity, gradually reduced his injection to the point where Lee started to relapse again. By the time they realized what was happening, he was in real trouble. When he saw a new psychiatrist (his usual one having just retired), Lee tried to explain that he was having all the same symptoms that he had suffered during his schizophrenic breakdown. In a ward-round situation, this doctor asked him a couple of times why he chose to assume that his present problems were caused by a previous illness. I do not suppose that most of us would be well equipped to answer such a question, but Lee tried! He was becoming more and more vulnerable and by the end of the interview he was floundering and frustrated. The doctor decided that the young man was exhibiting signs of inadequacy, probably because he was unable to cope with full-time employment, and suggested that he should take a break from this and resume attending a day-care resource for a few weeks. Later, the officer in charge decided that this sort of inadequacy should not be encouraged and that it would be a mistake to readmit this young man; the doctor did not argue the point.

To sum up Lee's sad story, the neuroleptic medication that enabled him to make his recovery was reduced to the point of ineffectiveness, *although he was keeping marvellously well on the original dose.* His accurate interpretation of what was happening to him was ignored by a psychiatrist who did not know the young man and who chose not to listen to what he was actually saying. Finally, a senior health professional decided that he should not be encouraged in his inadequacy to cope in the world outside. Sadly, it is not uncommon for changes that indicate early, treatable signs of a schizophrenic relapse to be regarded as *behaviour* that needs to be ignored rather than *sickness* that requires urgent attention.

This all happened several years ago; eventually, the young man was readmitted to the day resource that turned its back on him earlier when skilled observation would quickly have confirmed that he was becoming psychotic. Much later still, he has failed to make the sort of recovery he so painstakingly achieved after his first breakdown. There are no signs at present that he will work again. This is just one example of how dependent even the best-adjusted sufferers are on those who prescribe their medication and on those who have the power to intervene before tragedy strikes. What a sobering responsibility!

AFTER-CARE

Most families grappling with schizophrenia in the home claim that, by the end of the 1980s, so-called 'community care' means nothing more than family care. Perhaps we can attempt to judge the merits of that claim by taking a look at the sort of service presently offered to the majority of sufferers, regardless of whether or not they have families to support them.

This chapter has looked at some, but by no means all, of the problems that can occur when there is a pressing need to get sufferers into hospital either for a first breakdown or for later relapses. Once in there, they are hopefully stabilized on new or adjusted medication. Because of the acute and escalating shortage of beds at this time, patients increasingly tend to be discharged sooner rather than later. This is often after only a few weeks and frequently before they or any informal carers feel able to cope, putting a premium on those at home developing the necessary skills to cope with the individual's very real vulnerability and any remaining symptoms. But what, then, of sufferers who have no available family to return to? Only a small proportion can be found sheltered accommodation and many are discharged to an isolated bedsit or, too frequently, to some seedy 'bed and breakfast' establishment. At best, then, premature discharge puts a great strain on a family trying to support a recovering sufferer. At worst, the patient is discharged to circumstances that the rest of us would find trying and difficult when well.

It is hardly surprising that discharge from hospital can often be the start of a further relapse. Jan, an intelligent, middle-aged woman who has now learned to protect herself and to keep well, commented recently that she is inclined to see her four relapses and hospitalizations over the first six years of her illness as extensions of the first severe breakdown from which she had not really recovered by the time she was discharged. This echoes claims that I have heard from countless others and yet Jan acknowledges that she was able to spend longer in hospital during her first illness than sufferers are able to do nowadays. She therefore fears for their chances of recovering well enough to resume a normal lifestyle. Her concern is perhaps borne out by statistics for the late 1980s which seem to indicate that first-time admissions for schizophrenia account for only one in ten of all admissions for this illness.[21] Such figures may reflect a reluctance to diagnose first episodes, but they also must point to many sufferers becoming victims of the 'revolving door' syndrome. Clearly, early discharge is not the only factor here. Increasingly, many individuals are now losing out on even the basics of comfort – warmth and enough to eat – in what remains of our welfare state. In these circumstances, standards of professional care are becoming a vitally important factor in their chances of survival in the community.

In a recent London survey of 100 ex-psychiatric hospital patients,[22] sixty-one said that no one had discussed their potential welfare benefits with them before they left hospital, and forty-three had encountered a range of problems in claiming benefits after leaving hospital. Interestingly, those likely to be most in need of help, that is, those moving into a single housing unit or emergency accommodation, received the least assistance. Fifty-five of the sample had day care or other activities arranged for them before leaving hospital, and a similar number reported that their medication was not discussed with them prior to their discharge. One of the others said, 'Nobody was concerned to help me; I was advised to see my GP about drugs, *but I haven't got one*' (my italics). A number of patients specifically mentioned difficulties in managing their drugs and wanted help with this. Eighty of the sample were dissatisfied with their housing arrangements, and the nature of their complaints tended to reflect the poor standard of housing so often available to this under-privileged section of the population.

This survey reflects the findings of reports in different parts of the country. Research conducted in Essex in 1988, for example, showed that almost two-thirds of the discharged patients studied had received no advice at all on leaving hospital.[23] The potential recovery of psychiatric patients is undermined not only by difficulties of getting into and staying in hospital but also by the absence of any satisfactory procedure before their discharge to ensure that they are equipped to cope with the essentials once back in the community. At one end of the scale, there are plenty of examples of good practice, with community psychiatric nurses (CPNs) in particular keeping in touch with more vulnerable discharged sufferers, persevering with efforts to motivate them to take part in stimulating day care activities where these are available, and calling at the home to give a regular injection. Some of those unsupported by loved ones can survive with this amount of attention but their quality of life will depend on the determined efforts of those working with them. However, there are few, if any, health professionals who have the time to maintain the level of support that some sufferers need, such as making foolproof arrangements for ensuring they get up in the morning to take advantage of any resources being offered! Even where very caring programmes are initiated by dedicated workers in the community, it is rare indeed that the impetus can be maintained indefinitely without some sort of continuing support *within the living situation*, such as can be provided by families or residential staff. At the other end of the scale, there are health authorities which have no community psychiatric nurses at all and others which are content to let their CPNs work on an open referral system in which they *choose their own caseload*. As many find working with chronic mental illness both demanding and unrewarding, it may not be surprising that they tend to avoid it when the choice is left to them! Where such a system operates, there is a pronounced tendency for such professionals to choose to work with individuals who suffer with mild neurotic-type symptoms provoked by the pressures of everyday life; a new client population increasingly referred to as the 'worried well'. Predictably, a scarce resource then becomes even less available for the seriously mentally ill.

For many vulnerable sufferers, then, even the obtaining of the two basic essentials, that is, their medication and their welfare benefits, can only be achieved if they are able and motivated enough to organize themselves into attending a clinic regularly at a prescribed time, and if they learn to cope with the awe-inspiring intricacies of the social security regulations. One member of the National Schizophrenia Fellowship who befriended a young man trying to cope in the community reported:

When I asked about Ian's failure to receive his supplementary benefit for several weeks, I found this had happened because he had not signed on at the correct time on one occasion and it took several weeks before the new claim was authorized. The journey to the Unemployment Benefit office where he had to sign on was quite long and awkward; he experienced considerable difficulty getting there.[24]

Thus, being vulnerable in the first place puts one very much at risk of becoming more vulnerable because of the unrealistic expectations of the system! Families so often find that persuading their relatives to persevere with claiming their benefits and with attending clinics for their injections is a constant hassle, compounded by both the inertia of the illness and the apparent lack of flexibility and understanding of those providing the services. If there are constant problems for those sufferers who remain handicapped but who have families behind them, is it any wonder that so many more isolated sufferers are increasingly 'slipping through the net'? In the 'news release' that accompanied a recent publication with this title, the Director of the National Schizophrenia Fellowship stated:

People with schizophrenia and others who are seriously mentally ill are being put out of hospital into the community supposedly with a safety net of services to support them, but the reality is that the community care and support services barely exist if they exist at all. Consequently, thousands of people are slipping through the net with tragic results.[25]

SUMMING UP

We are discussing a common, treatable illness that is one of the most serious known to man, and yet the experiences of many sufferers point to a failure to take initial preventive measures to protect them from the worse ravages of the illness. Later signs of predictable relapse are denied. The witness of those closest to sufferers is often ignored until the time has passed when the latter will accept help. Some professionals also deny the sensible claims of sufferers themselves that their psychotic symptoms are returning. At best, the great hopes of an 'open door' policy in the 1950s and 1960s have led to a 'revolving door' syndrome where many sufferers' lives are punctuated by crisis admissions to hospital which are too often traumatic for all concerned. At worst, many of those who would previously have spent the rest of their lives in hospital are actually perishing out in the community. Instead of 'open doors', we have rapidly closing doors with sick people being turned away from the asylum they need. Instead of acceptance, acknowledgment and preventive care, we have continuing denial. Perhaps it is time for us to look for explanations for the prevailing attitudes which have contributed so much to this depressing state of affairs?

5 · Some Ideas and Theories

Although Sigmund Freud warned that psychosis would turn out to be of physical origin, and eventually abandoned all attempts to work with schizophrenia himself, some of his followers thought differently and claimed that the condition was a result of traumatic early childhood experiences. Meanwhile, alongside the enthusiastic growth of such ideas, other very different theories were being researched, and by the start of the Second World War impressive evidence was accumulating to show that there was a genetic element in schizophrenia, with blood relatives of sufferers having significantly raised chances of having the illness themselves, whether or not they lived together. Thus began the 'nature vs. nurture' debate that has raged ever since.

For some years after the war, this debate became rather one-sided as most thinking people instinctively recoiled from the sort of geneticist ideas which had become associated with Naziism. Perhaps we can begin to gauge just how much this emotive subject may have slowed down objective reasoning and research by the following comment from a clinical psychologist, David Pilgrim, in the *New Statesman forty-three years* after the reign of Naziism. This was in response to a protest by the Director of the National Schizophrenia Fellowship that research has clearly and consistently shown there to be an inherited aspect to this illness:

I can . . . supply her with evidence that the bias towards genetic reasoning about 'schizophrenia' was started by German eugenicists during the Nazi period. Are the National Schizophrenia Fellowship proud to uphold such a tradition?[1]

If such sentiments can be expressed so vehemently in the late 1980s after half a century of increasingly sophisticated evidence of a genetic component in this illness, maybe it is not so surprising that environmental theories became so popular during the post-war years. Such strong feelings combined with the medical profession's significant lack of success in treating the illness made it inevitable that there would be a move away from a medical model of schizophrenia after the war. The influence of psychoanalysts led to the 'family theories' of schizophrenia and to the growth of the anti-psychiatry movement, both of which flourished throughout the 1960s and 1970s.

THE FAMILY THEORIES

By the late 1940s, psychoanalysts were focusing their attention on the parenting of a child, claiming that poor mothering was the factor which led to the development of schizophrenia. A new phrase entered the English language – the 'schizophrenogenic mother' (that is, a mother *causing schizophrenia*).[2] Depending on the school of thought, mothers were described as cold, hostile, domineering, over-protective or over-involved. Before very long, many health professionals working in this field, including some doctors and psychiatrists, were regarding schizophrenia as a condition brought about by faulty parenting. Two leading British psychiatrists commented on this phenomenon:

It is above all the mothers who are condemned. They have shown either excessive strictness, or excessive indulgence. They have been indecisive and ambivalent, or have shown a covert harshness and moral inflexibility . . . they have shown either a cool detachment or an excessive devotion. It is difficult to resist the conclusion that we are being offered an account of mothers who by and large are within the normal range of human variation, but who are very much mother. It seems to have been their maternity even more than their humanity which has aroused so much indignation.[3]

The fact that most of these mothers also had normal non-schizophrenic children seemed to raise no doubts for the proponents of this sort of theory, as the phenomenon was rationalized by claims that the mother's attitude towards the potential sick child was different, and that this was provoked by one of various factors, such as her health during the pregnancy, the child's birthweight, the position of the child in the family, or whatever. Fortunately for the theorists, and less so for mothers, these sorts of factor are unarguable, albeit probably also irrelevant. In fact for a quarter of a century, parents of schizophrenia sufferers could not win. They were the scapegoats for the very tragedies which in so many cases devastated their family lives. Colin Blakemore, the author of *The Mind Machine*, has commented: 'To lose a child to schizophrenia is a tremendous load to bear. To be told that this awful disorder is due to the way the child was nurtured is far worse.'[4]

In the mid-1950s, in the fervent search for evidence of 'sick' families rather than a disease entity we call schizophrenia, two Americans, Bateson and Jackson, introduced their concept of the 'double bind' communication,[5] and this was to become everyday jargon in psychiatry for over two decades. The 'double bind' is a communication which conveys two contradictory messages, as, for example, in 'Come and give me a cuddle – oh, you've spoilt my new hairdo!' The child eagerly runs up to cuddle mother and then finds this does not please; a 'no-win' situation. It was claimed that families undermined and confused the member who would eventually become schizophrenic by conveying mixed messages. But the studies which led to this theory were based on these workers' observation of the communication in families *where a member had just been recognized by the experts as being schizophrenic*, that is, they observed the communication between family members once the illness had manifested itself, and found this to be abnormal. For example, picture the impression that might have been gained by an outsider (who disregarded a 'disease model' explanation of schizophrenia) in an interview with a young sufferer like Steven and his family before medication calmed him, as described in Chapter 1. He would still be suffering the terror of his delusional ideas, and his parents would be trying to communicate their desperate need for help without in any way further antagonizing a sick son.

Despite all the seemingly obvious dangers of drawing conclusions about the usual everyday behaviour of any individual during a time of such anguish, the concept of the 'double bind' was adopted zealously by academics and health professionals alike. (This zeal has faded away during the 1980s with the gradual, belated realization that although the 'double bind' is an interesting feature of human communications, it is of no more relevance to families with schizophrenia than to the rest of the population.) There followed a proliferation of similar theories concentrating on the supposed abnormalities within the families of schizophrenia sufferers. In particular, the work of one American, Lidz, on relationships within these families was widely quoted. His theory was that the relationship between the parents of sufferers was distorted, with one spouse abnormally dominant over, or cold and hostile towards the other, with the resulting sick family presenting their scapegoated member as 'schizophrenic'. Such ideas proved to be remarkably pervasive, so much so that one still occasionally hears a professional referring to the 'presenting patient', with the implication that he or she may not be the sick member of the family. It has been pointed out that Lidz once observed that about half of all schizophrenics had mothers who were 'strange, near-psychotic or even overtly schizophrenic', and earlier he described fathers of schizophrenics as exerting 'an extremely noxious or pathogenic influence upon the family and the patient'.[6] In retrospect, it is interesting that theories so lacking in both respect and compassion for fellow human beings in distress should have proved so popular. Predictably, other workers' attempts to replicate these sorts of finding were no more successful than those with the 'double bind'.

Early in the 1960s, Wynne and Singer in the United States[7] claimed that the causes of schizophrenia could be found in abnormal communication patterns within families with this illness and that they could detect which families had a schizophrenic member by the type of communication observed in the parents. Their claims excited interest for a time and their work was widely quoted and credited, but two attempts by Hirsch and Leff in Britain to replicate these findings failed,[8,9] and interest in the original work faded. Meanwhile, another researcher, Liem, found that any communication problems found amongst the parents were likely to be in response to abnormal messages from the sick child,[10] a seemingly logical observation echoed in an incidental finding of Wynne and Singer that *adoptive parents* of schizophrenic children demonstrated the same communication problems![11]

After a careful and detailed review of the above and other similar studies, two American psychologists, Neale and Oltmanns, concluded in 1980 that:

the double-bind concept has proved to be too elusive to measure reliably, and the notions associated with cold, domineering mothers and parental role reversals have not been confirmed . . . several recent studies suggest that the parents' difficulties may be a response to the stress of living with a seriously disturbed child.[12]

In retrospect, it scarcely seems credible that so much valuable time, effort and funding was focused on such barren terrain. Perhaps the most surprising feature of the research carried out with families with schizophrenia during these years was the seeming ignorance of the researchers in two areas which were fundamental to their work. First, there is no evidence of any understanding of human behaviour at times of crisis (years later, work with mass disasters is leading to a better appreciation of such matters) and second, there is no evidence of any basic knowledge about the behaviour of families in general. Indeed, one critic has pointed out that a serious defect in most family studies is that these tend to classify as 'pathological' certain patterns of communication 'which, far from being specific to schizophrenic families, are in fact commonplace and found in many families'.[13] Perhaps we should not be too surprised that neither psychoanalysis nor the family theories have contributed anything of significance to our understanding of schizophrenia. More seriously, they undoubtedly escalated the suffering of families trying to cope with this illness and they certainly contributed to the growth of a powerful movement which swept through Europe during the 1960s and 1970s and which continues to have enormous influence even today; the anti-psychiatry lobby. If schizophrenia was something that happened to a scapegoated member of a family because of faulty relationships and communication in the rest of the unit, then it couldn't be an illness, could it? As this was the most common serious disorder treated by psychiatrists, where did that leave psychiatry?

The anti-psychiatry movement emanated from the United States where the psychoanalytic and family theories were most dominant. On the one hand, psychoanalysts and an increasing number of mental health professionals were regarding schizophrenia as a type of escapist behaviour and, on the other, institutions were being blamed for perpetuating that behaviour. In the 1960s

Ervin Goffman wrote his much acclaimed book, *Asylums*. From his experience of working in a large hospital in Washington, DC for eighteen months, he claimed that some hospitals were 'total institutions' in which patients learned certain behaviours that helped them to live better and get along within that setting. That observation could perhaps be applied to most life situations, but he believed that most of the behaviour he noted in the patients was due to 'institutionalization'. In 1959, Russell Barton had coined the phrase 'institutional neurosis' in his book of the same name[14] and warned of the dangers of creating further pathology in the patient by the sorts of regime he frequently found in hospitals. There is little doubt that at the time these authors were writing, there were plenty of examples of 'bad' institutions, and during the next fifteen years or so these became very much the focus of attention as one scandal after another hit the headlines. These concerned the neglect or abuse of patients in some of the large old hospitals for the mentally handicapped and the mentally ill; in such a climate it was no wonder that the public were ready to believe that the old hospitals should be abandoned. In fact, Goffman did not deny the existence of 'good' institutions, and it was rather typical of the psychiatry debate at that time that the campaigning became an 'all or nothing' exercise, and no attempt was made to identify any positive features of the meaning of the word 'asylum'. There was total rejection of institutions in any form. Such ideas have had a profound effect on both policy and attitudes. Nowadays medical teams regularly discharge reluctant and chronically ill sufferers after only a few weeks' stay in hospital following acute breakdown, telling them that otherwise they may become 'institutionalized'. But, as Kathleen Jones has pointed out, the symptoms of 'institutional neurosis' – submissiveness, apathy and shuffling gait – are indistinguishable from the symptoms of a chronic schizo-phrenic illness,[15] as can be seen in tragically damaged young sufferers who have never had more than one or two short admissions to hospital.

Goffman was one of several exponents of the 'labelling theory', which was to become of increasing significance to those unfortu-nate enough to develop a schizophrenic illness, as any attempt at diagnosis in mental illness would come to be regarded as 'labelling' and, therefore, punitive. According to this argument, mental illness is nothing more than a label attached to a *deviant form of behaviour* that is inconvenient to society. Once labelled, the individual has no choice but to adhere to this behaviour, and attached to the label is a stigma from which he or she cannot escape. A group of words such as labelling, stigma, scapegoating and institutionalization became the hallmark of the anti-psychiatry movement. The argument went something like this: society, and the family in particular, scapegoats one of its members who is presented as the patient, and whose behaviour then becomes labelled as mentally ill, confirming his or her deviant status. This behaviour is then reinforced and escalated by society, and by psychiatrists in particular, with the use of drug treatment and institutionalization. Thus families, psychiatrists and hospitals were held to blame for the nightmare world of the schizophrenia sufferer. The proponents of such ideas did not recognize that schizophrenia involves profound suffering in its own right, and frequently claimed that schizophrenia was a form of escape from the harsh realities of the world. Ronald Laing, the main British proponent of the 'double bind' theory, wrote in the 1970s: 'Without exception, the experience and behaviour that gets labelled schizophrenic is a special strategy that a person invents in order to live in an unliveable situation.'[16]

Most sufferers would not regard their illness as a strategy for survival. Nor would they describe their lives before schizophrenia as unliveable; for many it was a period of excitement and achievement that can only be experienced in the prime of life. And yet, Laing was to become the idol of many professionals and of most social work courses in the United Kingdom, and his views on the subject may well be summed up by his statement that 'schizophrenia is the name for a condition that most psychiatrists ascribe to patients they call schizophrenics'.[17] This, of course, was music to the ears of those professionals who were becoming increasingly resistant to a medical model of serious mental illness.

Perhaps the most influential of all the anti-psychiatry leaders has been Dr Thomas Szasz in the United States, who continues to claim that mental illness is a myth, apparently perpetuated by psychiatrists to further their own interests. A psychiatrist himself, it seems that he does not acknowledge any illness other than the recognized physical disorders. It follows, therefore, that diagnosing individuals as mentally ill and admitting them to hospital is a violation of their dignity and liberty. Such ideas proved most attractive to civil liberty lobbies right across the world and they do not seem to have balked at the less palatable side of Szasz's philosophy; whereas he opposes the idea that people exhibiting mad behaviour should be admitted to hospital for treatment, he seemingly maintains that if such behaviour becomes anti-social then they should become subject to the law of the land in the same way as everyone else. Thus the civil liberty movement has embraced a dogma which frowns on the idea of incarceration in hospitals for the purposes of treatment and protection of individuals at times of sickness, but not on their incarceration in prisons for the purposes of punishment.

And so the ideas of the 1960s and 1970s, far removed from the urgent needs of individuals with a serious mental illness and of their families, went from strength to strength. Governments in several countries, always looking to save money, were happy to be persuaded that mental illness would fade away if there were no institutions in which to perpetuate it. They made strange and uneasy alliances with a civil liberty movement made up of various fringe movements, some of them political and extreme left-wing in nature, all calling for the closing of the mental hospitals and the discharge of their patients into a supposedly welcoming community. At its most extreme the anti-psychiatry movement has produced a political climate which facilitated the passing of a law in Italy precluding new admissions to hospital after 1978 and a relentless surge towards the closing of mental hospitals in many other parts of the world.

The anti-psychiatry movement's emphasis on the evils of labelling and institutionalization are still dominant in much of the work carried out with the mentally ill, and especially so with schizophrenia. Sufferers with the acute form of the illness need health professionals who are not over-influenced by theories on labelling and stigma, and who recognize that their urgent requirement is for prompt recognition of threatened breakdown or relapse and for preventive treatment. Similarly, many sufferers have an intermittent but real need for asylum and this is becoming less and less available with the closing of the hospitals. Finally, the most vulnerable 10 per cent have an ongoing need for asylum and, as we enter the last decade of the twentieth century, some of these are now being turned away.

CONTEMPORARY IDEAS

Although relatively little is heard these days of the leaders of the anti-psychiatry movement who were so vocal in the 1960s and 1970s, there have been recent attempts by several British psychologists to revive the idea that 'Schizophrenia is a myth'. David Hill, Director of Camden MIND, is seemingly the main spokesman in the media for a largely abandoned cause. In response to reports of early but promising work in the search for an offending gene, he wrote in the *New Statesman* in August 1988:

Schizophrenia was invented around the turn of the century . . . The original list of symptoms – and there are hundreds of them – included: 'They conduct themselves in a free and easy way, laugh on serious occasions, are rude and impertinent towards their superiors, challenging them to duels; they go about in untidy and dirty clothes, unwashed, unkempt, go with a lighted cigar into church, speak familiarly to strangers, and decorate themselves with gay ribbons . . .' Today, as then, 'schizophrenia remains nothing more than an endless list of broken social norms.'[18]

Any attempt at responsible debate would surely have included some of the crippling and unique features of a schizophrenic illness? Judith Weleminsky, Director of the National Schizophrenia Fellowship, replied:

A quarter of a million people in Britain today suffer from schizophrenia and people like David Hill increase the misery of them and their families by denying the reality of this severely disabling illness.[19]

Another latter-day proponent of a similar theme is David Pilgrim, the psychologist quoted earlier who criticizes any attempt to demonstrate the genetic component in schizophrenia seemingly because of the Nazi regime's preoccupation with such matters. He advances the idea that the concept of schizophrenia as an entity is maintained only by four parties with a vested interest in this and suggests these are:

(a) *Psychiatrists*, supposedly to retain the mandate to manage this particular 'form of deviance'.

(b) *Drug companies*, supposedly for economic reasons.

(c) The rest of his own profession of *clinical psychologists*, supposedly to maintain the division, whereby psychiatry is concerned with psychosis and psychology with neurosis.

(d) The *relatives*, because 'madness' is offensive and disruptive to the 'non-mad'.

He concludes that, 'an honest re-appraisal of the nature of schizophrenia is required. However, the four vested interests I highlight above are very likely to impede the progress of this exercise.'[20]

Interestingly, despite the implications in his comments under (a) and (c), some members of David Pilgrim's own profession of clinical psychology are very much involved in valuable research and in pioneering successful ways of working with schizophrenia.[21] Perhaps Pilgrim and his colleagues might do well to heed the invitation of a leading psychiatrist and researcher in this field: 'Instead of battering at an open door, [they] should come in and make their contribution.'[22]

ANOTHER FAMILY THEORY

The latest of the family theories is the 'high expressed emotion' theory, which started to take shape during the 1970s at about the time all the others were dying. It differs from the earlier theories in that there is no suggestion that the family unit is a possible cause of schizophrenia, but rather that it can influence the course of the illness for those sufferers whose illness is severe enough to make them 'revolving door' patients. As we have already seen, the course of schizophrenia is similar to that of other degenerative disorders such as multiple sclerosis and Parkinson's disease, in that there is a pattern of remission and relapse.

In 1972, attention once more focused on the home environment, and Brown and his colleagues interviewed families *immediately their relative had been admitted to hospital following yet another relapse* and 'measured' levels of what they called 'expressed emotion' in terms of critical comment and hostility and also over-protectiveness, which was described as emotional 'over-involvement'. They found that in households where there were high levels of such 'expressed emotion', sufferers were more likely to relapse.[23] In 1976, Vaughn and Leff replicated this work and found that 58 per cent of patients in 'high expressed emotion' families suffered a relapse, as against 16 per cent of patients in 'low expressed emotion' families.[24] Before very long, 'high expressed emotion' had become part of psychiatric jargon.

In 1986, I discussed the interpretation of the findings of this research critically and in some detail,[25] pointing out, for example, that the 58 per cent of patients who relapsed tended to be those who had excessive periods of 'face-to-face' contact with carers; this may well mean that these individuals are the very ones that cannot be catered for or even 'contained' in any day care resources *because of the severity of their illness*. We are very much into a 'chicken and egg' type situation here; the level of 'high expressed emotion' found in the family may well reflect the level of the difficulties provoked by the sufferer's condition, and, of course, the level of back-up support being received. Such research may be revealing more about the dire circumstances such families are trying to cope with, than any factor that is relevant to risk of relapse in the sufferer. Not surprisingly, it is now being realized that 'high expressed emotion' is a feature found not only in some relatives of people who suffer from schizophrenia, but also from an increasing list of other conditions such as depression, manic depressive illness, anorexia, mental handicap, Parkinson's disease and senile dementia. Indeed, Kuipers and Bebington point out: 'While much theoretical and clinical interest remains in the use of "EE" in schizophrenia, the measure itself appears to tap difficulties common to the care of many disabling problems.'[26]

Similarly, there is a growing recognition that high levels of expressed emotion can also be found in *professionals* working closely with seriously handicapped schizophrenic patients. One pilot study carried out in three general psychiatric wards in West Germany found that at least 62 per cent of nurses showed high expressed emotion with regard to patients being discussed and that 'many of the problems expressed and emotions experienced by the nurses bear striking resemblance of those of family members and other close relations of patients'.[27] Clearly, whatever we may think we are measuring when we assess levels of 'expressed emotion', we are certainly receiving feedback on the amount of stress experienced by those who care.

Meanwhile, in 1985, MacMillan and his colleagues at North-wick Park Hospital looked closely at the phenomenon of 'high expressed emotion' in families with schizophrenia and warned that their findings cast 'considerable doubt on speculations that import-ant predictions of outcome are prevalent in the family environ-ment'[28] and, more recently, work on a long-term study in Nithsdale in South-West Scotland has failed to show any relationship at all between levels of 'expressed emotion' and relapse rates.[29]

As time passes, it seems that we are learning once more that a factor which has been 'discovered' and linked specifically with families with schizophrenia is actually a normal part of human behaviour that can be witnessed under certain types of stress.

A STRESS-RELATED DISORDER?

The 'high expressed emotion' theory is based on the widespread belief that schizophrenia is a stress-related disorder. Many years of observing the way in which most sufferers cope with day-to-day problems which most healthy people would find overwhelming have made me sceptical of such a view. And I am not alone in my cynicism about the emphasis laid on stress by many writers and workers in this field. It has frequently been pointed out that there is no increased incidence of schizophrenia in situations where human beings are living under dire stress, for example, in prisoner-of-war camps, in concentration camps, in populations surviving disasters such as earthquakes and in those living in cities under constant threat of bombing.[30]

A British psychiatrist, Brenda Lintner, has recently commented:

The characteristic of most stress-related illnesses is that they improve when the stress is removed, whereas most schizophrenic illnesses do not.

Someone with a depression related to environmental problems may well become much better when admitted to hospital for a short time and then become worse when they go home, even for a weekend. This rarely happens in a schizophrenic condition, as could be observed in the days before any effective treatment existed.[31]

Undue emphasis on stress can lead to the seeking of external explanations for problems which would otherwise be seen as signs of abnormality in the individual. Professionals have tended to explain away such problems as being derived from the frustrations of everyday living instead of querying why they should suddenly produce symptoms which are causing concern. An over-simplified and often irrelevant equation seems to have become the rule by which some of them work:

DECIDE WHAT THE STRESS FACTOR IS AND REMOVE IT = GOOD HEALTH!

This is non-productive in a developing or relapsing schizophrenic illness as it merely delays the response to the need for urgent treatment.

Clearly, too much stress *as perceived by the individual* is not good for anyone in good or poor health, but stress, as perceived by the onlooker, may well be irrelevant, and particularly so where schizophrenia is concerned. Once a schizophrenic illness is established, many sufferers learn what situations stress them and how to protect themselves; for example, some will avoid the responsibilities associated with promotion at work while others will seek such challenges as a way of combating feelings of boredom with which they cannot cope. Similarly, more handicapped individuals may find a lot of noise and activity around them unacceptable in view of the bombardment of stimuli with which they already have to cope. Others will be stressed by a change of ward or establishment, or a change of staff, or by a lack of opportunity for privacy and space. It is to be expected that individuals with health problems of any kind will feel the need to protect themselves from certain factors in their environment which they find unhelpful or stressful, but this does not necessarily indicate that their original condition is a stress-related one.

SUMMING UP

I have looked at some of the psychoanalytic and family theories that have abounded in the handling of schizophrenia and at the anti-psychiatry lobby with its emphasis on labelling, scapegoating, stigma and institutionalization. Over the course of two decades, academics and professionals alike were prepared to point an accusing finger at families and label them sick without offering any explanation as to what that meant or what had caused it. Similarly, those who deplored the diagnosis of mental illness as the *scapegoating* of an individual by his or her family, had no compunction about scapegoating other individuals who happened to be mothers, fathers, husbands, wives, brothers or sisters. Furthermore, civil liberty lobbies have gladly embraced a movement which wanted to stop the treatment of patients in hospital but which claimed that such patients should be given the dignity of being regarded as normal, with the right to be put into another sort of institution – a prison – if their behaviour unwittingly offends society.

How have these far-reaching ideas affected the treatment and policies surrounding schizophrenia? The contradictions inherent in the ideas so far discussed tend to be echoed in the attitudes and goals of many of those involved with working with schizophrenia. Sadly, this has resulted in creating a real 'mad hatter's tea party' that has little to do with the illness itself.

6 · Muddled Thinking

In what ways have the ideas and theories discussed in the last chapter influenced the fate of people with schizophrenia in the United Kingdom?

There were immediate repercussions early in the 1960s when a Tory government was quick to take advantage of a situation in which the new drug treatment had made it possible to discharge so many hospital patients into the community and in which the ideology of the day was proclaiming that mental illness was the product of institutionalization. Enoch Powell, the then Minister of Health, announced the start of the closure of the mental hospitals, and it was not long before claims were being made that this could be completed by the mid-1970s. Within a few years, the politically active pressure group MIND (the National Association for Mental Health) became the unlikely ally of successive governments attempting to carry out the proposed closure programme. But this was proving less simple than had originally been imagined. Indeed, before very long everyone except, perhaps, for those intent on closing the hospitals, was becoming uncomfortably conscious of a new phenomenon; the 'long-stay' patient was being replaced by the 'revolving door' patient and hospital admissions were not decreasing in the way that had been forecast. Meanwhile, MIND, by far the most influential pressure group in mental health for several decades, has constantly propounded a determined and confident view that the mentally ill will fare better without the hospitals if funding is made available for appropriate resources in the community. Despite an alarming absence of any measures being taken by successive governments to ensure the speedy provision of even modest community resources, MIND's policy-makers have nevertheless kept up a relentless clamour for a more rapid closure of the hospitals. During the same period a shortage of hospital beds has coincided with a growing population of the mentally ill in our prisons and on our streets. The ideologies of the 1960s and 1970s have indeed proved to be very pervasive, and the real and urgent needs of people suffering from schizophrenia and other psychotic conditions may well have been sacrificed in the pursuit of unproven and unresearched theories.

LEGISLATION

MIND engaged an American lawyer, Larry Gostin, to advocate on their behalf in the discussions that led to the drawing up of the Mental Health Act 1983. He brought with him to Britain a considerable experience of civil liberty issues in his own country and he had a profound influence on the spirit of this new legislation. The move of emphasis from *enabling* to *avoiding* treatment in hospitals nicely complements the drive to close down these institutions, and it may be significant that the Mental Health Act 1983 has been described as 'an eviction order for schizophrenics'.[1] Indeed, the current trend to emphasize 'negative rights' rather than 'positive rights' is echoed in this legislation and in the way it is interpreted. Kathleen Jones explains these terms:

Rights for; positive rights to a decent quality of life, a home, a job, care and treatment when we need it, have been ignored, while the emphasis has been placed on negative rights; the right *not* to be categorized as mentally ill, *not* to be committed to hospital, *not* to receive treatment. Too often, for chronic patients, this means the right to live at the bottom of the heap.[2]

When individuals are actively psychotic they do not appreciate that they are ill and in need of treatment. It is usually left to those most concerned with them to seek help urgently, only to find that the professionals who come to assess relapsing sufferers may be fooled by their desperate attempts to deceive and reassure. Even when it is clear to doctors or social workers that the individual is indeed very sick, they may still hesitate to use the law because there is a widespread belief amongst professionals working with the mentally ill that patients have to be a danger to themselves or to others before they can be formally admitted to hospital. In fact, the National Schizophrenia Fellowship and others fought hard for the words 'in the interests of his health' to be included as one of the grounds for admission under the Act. It is astonishing that many professionals who work with this legislation do not acknowledge this, and there is daily talk of very ill people being 'not sectionable yet', meaning they cannot be admitted under a section of the Mental Health Act 1983 because they are not obviously on the point of endangering themselves or others. The President of the Royal College of Psychiatrists has recently commented on this dilemma:

In England, Wales and Scotland it is possible to admit a person compulsorily solely on the grounds of 'health'. I regard this provision as highly desirable and indeed essential. Many patients who require treatment do not need to be admitted for the sake of their safety or safety of others, but to prevent further deterioration of their mental health.[3]

He then went on to discuss the balance that psychiatrists have to strive for in the interests of their patients' trust and confidence:

When I admit a patient compulsorily, on grounds of health alone, I try to act at a point when the patient recognizes, at some level, that he needs help. . . . I may have to wait for this point to be reached. If I wait too long, however, even if his health does not deteriorate further, his social reputation or his social network, whether of family, friends, neighbours or workmates, may be severely damaged or irretrievably broken.[4]

Indeed, everyone working with schizophrenia should be aware that unrelieved psychotic symptoms can cause irreversible damage to the individual's mental and physical health, career and relationships. Furthermore, it is quite common for sufferers when psychotic to be grappling with destructive instructions from their voices to jump off a high building, to run in front of a lorry or to take some other potentially fatal action.[5] Some do not succeed in resisting these compelling commands even though they may have no wish to kill themselves. It is not uncommon to come across survivors of such experiences who are permanently maimed as a result of them. A more insidious danger is a gradual and steady deterioration that leads to individuals with an unrelieved psychosis 'opting out' and neglecting themselves or taking to the streets. The mental health legislation can, and should, be used to avert these sorts of tragedy.

With the increasing shortage of beds, the complicated procedures required by the legislation, and the way it is regularly misinterpreted, it is really no wonder that it is becoming more and more difficult to obtain help for sufferers at times of crisis. Confirming the sort of trauma this causes, Detective Superintendent Tom Williamson of the Metropolitan Police has commented:

As police officers we can probably identify with some of the problems that families experience because we ourselves quite often get caught up in the bureaucratic nightmare of trying to refer the people that we get involved with to the hospital . . . one of the disasters in this whole area is the 'revolving door' patients because we see these people coming back in and out, getting worse and worse . . .[6]

In retrospect, it seems remarkable that so much time, effort and influence was dedicated to the sorts of reform that tend to increase the likelihood of seriously ill people 'dying with their rights on'.[7] Meanwhile, important 'positive rights' have been neglected and agitation for proper community resources for the vast majority of the seriously mentally ill have lagged far behind the pursuit of 'negative rights'.

NORMALIZATION AND ADVOCACY

Since Larry Gostin's return to the United States and the implementation of the Mental Health Act 1983, 'normalization' has become a main focus of MIND and of many mental health professionals. The argument goes something like this: if you treat people as normal and give them the opportunity to live a normal life, then their mental health problems will become unimportant, or even fade away. This may be a useful concept if applied to people with neurotic-type symptoms provoked by an intolerable life situation, but when it is applied to those who suffer with an illness like schizophrenia, then it can be dangerous. Some sufferers will need very special help and opportunities to be able to have anything approaching a normal lifestyle. One example of 'normalization' is the idea discussed in the last chapter, that each individual should take responsibility for his own lifestyle and behaviour and expect to be punished if this offends. This may make sense if we are referring to someone well enough to make calculated decisions about whether or not to obey the law. It does not if it is applied to someone who is too ill to understand the implication of such a decision, let alone to make one. Similarly, some hostels with schizophrenic residents have a policy that they should be treated as 'normal' and be responsible for organizing their own medication, for deciding whether or not to go for injections and whether or not to go and see their doctor. This sort of policy ignores the fact that if such residents were 'normal', they would not need to live in such a hostel (and thus provide employment for its staff). Many schizophrenia sufferers fall by the wayside where there is such abdication of responsibility for vulnerable clients. Terry Hammond, a regional director of the National Schizophrenia Fellowship who was formerly involved in the provision of housing for vulnerable sections of the community, has commented:

Community care for the mentally ill is about helping very sick people who are just as sick in the community as they are in hospital. It is about sustaining them in the community at a level they can cope with and at a level they want to cope with. . . . All the talk about independence and normalization for many chronically ill is nothing more than to be condemned to a life of loneliness and isolation. That is what simple independence is about for a significant majority of the chronically ill.[8]

Another of MIND's concerns is *advocacy*. There is a growing interest in the provision of a 'friend' or 'advocate' for those people who may be unable to protect their own interests effectively. Similarly, the last few years have seen the emergence of several consumer groups such as Survivors Speak Out, and whose members are beginning to make themselves heard. The following comment in an article in MIND's publication, *Openmind*, is not untypical of the sorts of opinion being expressed. The author of these words describes herself as a 'mental health system survivor':

'Mental illness' is a value judgement on people's behaviour, and in a classist, racist, sexist society where money rules, it is an extremely powerful method of social control . . . if we cease to write off the distress and pain of others as 'sickness' with a biochemical explanation, we can no longer use terms which devalue other people's experiences and which reduce them to objects in order for us to feel safe and superior.[9]

The fact that such sentiments are frequently expressed by people who have at some time been treated for mental illness is surely an indictment of society's attitude to this subject and a measure of the sense of degradation they associate with the whole experience.

Another factor that sometimes underlies this sort of rejection of the term 'mental illness' can be a profound objection to the idea that the mind can be regarded as sick. Most of us appreciate the weaknesses and vulnerability of the sophisticated machine we call the body; from a very early age we learn that it can achieve all sorts of amazing feats, but that it can also very easily bleed, bruise or ache! We are not so sure about this thing we call the mind. For many, it is something quite sacrosanct; a part of us that equates with the 'soul', that may well, indeed, survive beyond the body. Perhaps the profound resistance to a serious mental illness such as schizophrenia is that such denial is the final bastion in defence of the spiritual part of ourselves being something other than a product of our genes and the intricate working of our brain cells. In contrast, for those who refer to ' "sickness" with a biochemical explanation', the mind is inseparable from the brain, and surely the most wondrous and perplexing part of a sophisticated machine. Colin Blakemore suggests that such a view does not reduce human beings to 'mere' machines, but 'celebrates the richness of the mechanism inside our heads – the machine that makes the mind'.[10]

This whole issue is a profoundly serious and important one to many people. Perhaps the feelings of two schizophrenia sufferers I have worked with polarize in an important way the continuum of ideas on the subject. One commented that she felt insulted and 'dehumanized' by the idea that the torment and confusion in her mind could be caused by sickness and relieved by a chemical. The other replied, after a long pause, that he had learned to appreciate the need for medication, as far from 'dehumanizing' him, it allowed him to function fully again as a human being.

Meanwhile, because so many articulate 'survivors' believe it is in the best interests of themselves and of those who have had similar experiences to deny the existence of mental illness, they tend to increase the horror and stigma for those who cannot escape the reality and pain of a serious mental illness. They also drive further into hiding the many individuals who keep well only so long as they continue with their drug treatment. Bill George is a well-recovered sufferer who lives abroad and who leads a normal lifestyle. He is aware of his vulnerability and has found that the way to survive did not lie in denying this and his own need for medical treatment. He comments:

I know from experience that the major tranquillizers can be a boon in the treatment of psychosis. . . . The tendency in the client movement to want to do away with psychiatry and the medical model of mental problems is not, in my opinion, in our own best interests.[11]

There are, of course, other equally articulate schizophrenia sufferers who wish to relay the same sort of message on behalf of all those who need both respect and treatment rather than denial. Some of them have started to make themselves heard as representatives of VOICES, another young consumer organization, run by schizophrenia sufferers for sufferers.

THE PROFESSIONALS

We have noted the quick reaction of politicians to the advent of the neuroleptic drugs and the ideologies of the 1960s, as well as the growing influence of civil liberty lobbies. More recently, emphasis has focused on 'normalization' and 'user advocacy', and these concepts have been taken on board by small but articulate consumer movements. How have all these developments affected those who work with schizophrenia?

Perhaps it is easier to understand the 'conspiracy of silence' surrounding the whole subject of schizophrenia if we bear in mind that many of the senior members of the health professions were trained during the 1960s and 1970s. They were reared on the psychoanalytical and family theories discussed in the last chapter; theories which led to what has been described as 'the flight from the medical model'.[12] These were indeed 'heady' times when the established hierarchy of medicine, in psychiatry at least, was challenged for the first time. With many psychiatrists themselves supporting theories that the most common serious disorder they treated was a condition brought about by faulty upbringing, where did that leave psychiatry? The time had to be ripe for other health professionals to challenge the supremacy of their medical colleagues. The past three decades have seen a long power struggle within the mental health professions; this is not yet resolved and, sadly, it has in no way helped the cause of schizophrenia sufferers. Already beleaguered by what Hugh Gurling has referred to as 'all sorts of theories which try to explain everything without explaining anything',[13] they have also had to contend with a determined denial of the existence of schizophrenia as a medical entity by some of the professionals who actually work with them.

Perhaps this will be clearer if we take a look at several of the disciplines in turn. The nursing profession is the one which has traditionally worked most closely with the doctors within a medical setting. However, the English and Welsh National Boards Training Syllabus of 1982 highlighted the need for *a change from a medical model to a social model*. One much recommended and popular psychiatric nursing textbook[14] quotes this in its preface and perhaps this is why there are just two fleeting references to schizophrenia in this particular book of 370 pages. In contrast, it devotes a whole chapter to 'Human Sexuality'.

Psychiatric nursing students can successfully complete a three-year training course without learning about the symptoms of schizophrenia in any depth at all. During the latter half of the 1980s, the use of the word has been discouraged in examination questions (and, by implication, in answers to those questions). Similarly, when a patient is admitted to hospital, emphasis is placed on providing a nursing care plan which is based on his or her apparent needs, *as indicated by any presenting problems*. Little, if any, account is taken of the diagnosis (regarded as the province of the medical profession and often seen as 'labelling'), and it is not unusual to find nurses on the ward who are ignorant of the diagnosis of an individual patient. And so the members of the profession most involved with schizophrenia sufferers can become qualified without having the remotest idea as to how it might feel to suffer from the illness and without, therefore, any explanation for the predictable behaviour of those who do. A seemingly crazy situation, which becomes more so when we learn that one of the most currently popular ways for nurses to work with mental illness is to use a behavioural approach, involving the attempted modification of unacceptable behaviour.

How can one work intelligently with such an approach without an explanation for the behaviour under focus? More importantly, is it fair to expect a professional to accept and understand what may be strange, or even offensive, behaviour without having an explanation for it? And without such acceptance and understanding, how can there be real empathy? Without such empathy, how can 'caring' be real and become healing? During the spring of 1988 I heard two trained psychiatric nurses make the same comment separately during the course of one week. They were each speaking about two different men, both of whom have suffered from chronic schizophrenia for some years. The comment? . . . 'Oh, him, all he wants is for someone to wait on him!' They were right. Both men had pleaded to be readmitted to hospital. Both wanted a rest from the uphill struggle to survive and both were rather more sick than usual. Neither of these otherwise well-meaning nurses had the slightest idea of the difficulties with which these men have to cope, day in and day out.

This, then, is just one example of a moderate 'anti-medical model' approach in practice, but one which can seriously affect the majority of schizophrenia sufferers at some time. Another example is that found in the training of social workers. Although their basic training has always included a component on the subject of mental illness, for many years Ronald Laing, the leading proponent of the 'double bind' theory in Britain (see page 83), was seemingly the idol of their course tutors. Many social workers have completed their training knowing a lot about the various psychoanalytical and family theories of schizophrenia and little, if anything, about the illness itself.

One of the more positive features of the Mental Health Act 1983 is its attempt once again to involve social workers with the mentally ill. Before the profession went 'generic' in the early 1970s, there were social workers who specialized in working with mental illness and who were known as mental welfare officers (MWOs). Their work earned the lasting respect of sufferers and their families. Since that time social workers have had little opportunity to concern themselves with the mentally ill. Those who are qualified to work with the current legislation are known as approved social workers (ASWs) and they have to undergo around seventy days' extra training. The content and quality of the training varies from department to department and I know newly trained ASWs who are not aware that the legislation they have trained to work with allows for the sectioning of a patient 'in the interests of his health'. Furthermore, a recent paper on assessing the value of ASW training found that social workers themselves did not feel they knew enough about the mentally ill and matters concerning the mentally ill.[15] This is certainly confirmed by the experiences of many families trying to cope with a schizophrenic illness.

The reasons for becoming ASWs are as varied as the quality of the different training courses; some social workers have a genuine desire to specialize in mental illness, others do it for purposes of career advancement, and others are more or less obliged to do so by their managers. Whatever the reason for opting to take up this work, most ASWs have very little opportunity at the present time to work with the mentally ill and their families other than at times of crisis. Many only do an occasional assessment for formal admission to hospital and this may be in connection with conditions such as dementia, depression or mania, as well as schizophrenia. At the present time most mental health assessments for compulsory admission to hospital take place as a last resort, on a one-off basis, and social workers may find a crisis like the one experienced by Steven's family. The psychotic individual's studied calm and plausibility contrast markedly with the family's near hysteria, and can seem to confirm any theories the social worker may have learned at college about sick families scapegoating their most vulnerable member and presenting him or her as 'the patient'. Some professionals do not yet recognize the distraught behaviour of the family as a normal reaction to a horribly abnormal situation. It has to be an irony that Social Services departments all over the country are currently teaching the rest of us about the need for counselling and support for the families caught up in *mass disasters*, such as the slaughter at the Hillsborough football ground in 1989, and yet seem unaware of the pain and misery of the daily round of *individual disasters* being experienced by thousands of families struggling with schizophrenia. Meanwhile, although ASWs often have no more time than the rest of their profession to work with and to understand the problems of the mentally ill, the decisions they are expected to make can have a profound effect on the lives of sufferers and their loved ones. I do not believe this is fair to their clients or to themselves.

Perhaps the most worrying aspect of the 'anti-medical model' movement is its effect on some of those actually practising medicine, and particularly if they came into psychiatry years after the advent of the neuroleptic drugs (see pages 52–8). Some find it hard to defend their brand of treatment in the current climate of derision by colleagues from other disciplines, and it is not uncommon to find hospital doctors who have become quite sceptical of the value of drug treatment for schizophrenia. Without the memory of the frustrations of the early years before neuroleptic medication became available, it may perhaps be too easy to become critical of the imperfection of drugs that have in fact changed the face of an illness almost too awful to contemplate. Paradoxically, their impact was such that they made possible the sorts of reform that have since threatened the psychiatrist's professional status! Meanwhile, the ambivalence of some psychiatrists about the precious tools they have inherited can have dire consequences for sufferers, both for new ones and for those who have found a quality of life which would have been unthinkable before the 1950s. All too often we now hear of cases of sudden and devastating relapse after years of good health. The individual is persuaded, or instructed, to reduce the dose of medication 'as you have kept well for so long', with predictable results.

Similarly, some psychiatrists will avoid a diagnosis of schizophrenia until such time as the new sufferer becomes so damaged that everyone finally acknowledges the presence of chronic sickness. Once, when I pleaded for treatment sooner rather than later for a previously able and well-adjusted young man who had become psychotic, one such doctor told me, 'You do not seem to understand the significance of a diagnosis of schizophrenia; it is a devastating label to give someone.' He then pronounced this previously stable young person to be a 'border-line personality disorder', a *dustbin* of a diagnosis and a *label* which many schizophrenia sufferers receive at some time during their careers as psychiatric patients and which most find offensive. After two more years without the appropriate drug treatment this young man became the most damaged schizophrenia sufferer I have yet met, and the doctor finally prescribed neuroleptic medication for him. He now has 'a devastating label' which is superfluous; his behaviour, his impoverished social skills and appearance say it all. Can it be that a reluctance to acknowledge an unpleasant truth is more important to a professional practising medicine than wanting to protect a patient from irreversible harm and wasted potential? I never noted this particular psychiatrist diagnose schizophrenia unless the patient could already be seen to be damaged. It seems that Roger Freeman, when Health Minister with special responsibility for mental illness, may have come across this phenomenon; he commented in the House of Commons during January 1990:

I have met a number of families who, to their great despair and amazement, have seen their children lapse into schizophrenia, sometimes diagnosed too late. The children spend time in and out of psychiatric hospitals and then perhaps relapse into a chronic condition.[16]

On a special 'That's Life' television programme in April 1989 on mental illness,[17] a NHS midwife who suffered a post-natal depression after the birth of her first baby, pinpointed an anomaly in this preoccupation with the avoidance of 'labelling'. She told millions of viewers that she had been devastated by her treatment in a modern psychiatric unit, where she had been offered no sympathy and no one to talk to, and no diagnosis, *but had been informally labelled* 'attention-seeking', 'hysterical' and the like. When she eventually discharged herself and sought help elsewhere she at last received sympathy, understanding and a *diagnosis*. With an explanation for what was happening to her, she was then able to regain some dignity as well as her previous good health. If we avoid the use of a diagnosis – that is, *an explanation for what is happening to the individual* – then we have to find other reasons for his or her behaviour. There can be little doubt that the labels which are currently used to describe the behaviour of sick individuals are far more offensive and degrading than the use of a diagnosis which tells us something about what sufferers are experiencing. With a diagnosis, there is dignity of a kind and a basis for understanding and self-respect. With derogatory and judgmental labels, there is none.

A mature and intelligent woman once told me sadly about the

only time she really wanted to die during the long years of her illness. Phyllis had a very successful career in London before her first breakdown in her late twenties. After each breakdown, she fought back and tried to sort out her life again, but not understanding the importance of her drug treatment at that time, she found herself back in hospital again and again. On the last occasion, many years ago, she knew that her father and sister were coming up shortly to see the psychiatrist and she had an overwhelming feeling of having failed everyone yet again. 'I wanted to die, oh, I wanted to die so much,' she told me quietly. As she sat there, her voices told her to 'play dead', to lie down on the floor and to will herself dead; they insisted she could do it. Even while Phyllis apologized to me rather shamefacedly for believing that it could work, she remembered clearly how she did believe it and did as instructed, concentrating hard on this tragic task. She thought it was working and felt an overwhelming relief that it would all be over soon, when she looked up and saw her sister's anxious eyes peering down at her. 'Take no notice,' said the doctor, walking Phyllis's relatives to the office, 'she's just being attention-seeking!' She has never forgotten the mortification she felt at that moment.

Such is the confusion and denial that has resulted from a preoccupation with the labelling theories in mental illness, that it is far easier to *lose* a diagnosis of schizophrenia than to obtain one. This works in two different ways. The first has been challenged by a well-recovered sufferer, who has recently been giving talks in various parts of the country on what it really feels like to have schizophrenia. She is incensed by the tendency of psychiatrists and their colleagues to change the original diagnosis of schizophrenia for those sufferers who later manage to make a success of their lives against all the odds. She says this is a denial of everything that has been achieved: 'There are always continuing symptoms. One copes with these and learns to live with them, only to have the self-help, the years of struggle and battle discounted by professionals.'[18] What a strange irony. Everyone involved with schizophrenia is frightened of it because it is seemingly incurable. However, anyone who demonstrates that it is *conquerable* is assumed to have been misdiagnosed! Meanwhile, most of those sufferers who are able eventually to resume and maintain a completely normal lifestyle are those who are only too aware of, and have ready proof of, their very real vulnerability.

More damaging and dangerous is the tendency to change the diagnosis when a sufferer continues to present real problems despite continuous attempts at treatment. Frustrated professionals start to talk about the resulting behaviour as a feature of the individual's personality rather than part of a schizophrenic illness, and a choice of *labels* such as 'behaviour disorder' and 'personality disorder' replace the *diagnosis* of schizophrenia.

One such instance I came across recently was concerned with a middle-aged sufferer with a history of several breakdowns over the years and relatively good health in between. After his last breakdown, he had seemingly sunk into a chronic illness and had no interest or motivation at all. His new psychiatrist decided that a lifetime's diagnosis had been inaccurate. He advised the sufferer's elderly mother that this behaviour was the result of her giving too much care and attention to her son, who had now decided to be ill and enjoy being nursed and fussed over all the time. So, after coping rather well with a schizophrenic illness during most of his adult life, this sufferer has now been denied his sick status when he needs it and his mother has been given to understand it is all her fault.

WHY DENIAL?

Here, then, is a condition with an almost constant incidence of 1 per cent of the population throughout all the very different societies of our world;[19] an illness which is so common that it justifies the employment of the majority of mental health professionals in its own right, and yet which is ignored or avoided by many of them. Marjorie Wallace, in her award-winning series in *The Times* in 1985, described schizophrenia as 'the forgotten illness'[20] and she was right. Everyone, it seems, is able to forget about schizophrenia except for its victims and their loved ones. But why should this apply to those who are paid to work with this population? Why is it that many of those who have the most opportunity to witness the suffering and waste of lives caused by schizophrenia should be seduced by a succession of theories attempting to prove it is a myth?

Perhaps the answer lies partly in the ideas expressed earlier in this chapter; our determination to protect the sanctity of the mind as something that is impervious to disease or injury. Perhaps the answer lies in our need to defend ourselves from the possibility that here is a fate that can overtake us all. Perhaps the answer lies partly, too, in the regrettable fact that many mental health workers have been denied any real knowledge or tools with which to attempt to work with the illness. Their training has been influenced by the sorts of idea discussed in the last chapter and has tended to be either a conspiracy of silence about schizophrenia or a long series of theories that lead nowhere. It has more often than not omitted even a basic discussion on the classic cluster of symptoms which we call schizophrenia, let alone made any attempt to analyse the sorts of problem and need raised by such symptoms for sufferers and for those trying to care for them. Furthermore, most mental health professionals believe that up to one-third of all cases recover spontaneously *without their help* and that the rest suffer varying degrees of permanent damage regardless of any intervention on their part. As we have seen, the very real possibility of a good recovery after some years of illness is often not really entertained; it is denied by the means of invalidating the original diagnosis.

All in all, this adds up to a situation where some key professionals believe that schizophrenia is the appropriate name for the dreadful damage they see in the most chronic forms of the illness and that nothing else merits the diagnosis. I frequently meet colleagues who are surprised when I suggest that working with schizophrenia can be very rewarding because it is so *eminently treatable*. Usually, they have not been given, nor have they sought, opportunities to talk with sufferers about their experience of a psychotic nightmare nor to hear about what it is like to live with residual symptoms of this nightmare. They do not know, therefore, how similar the meaning of such experiences can be for those who have them, nor how stoic and *sensible* their coping mechanisms can be.[21] Similarly, it is depressingly rare to find professionals who have talked at any length with families having to struggle with schizophrenia in the home and so gained from hearing about their around-the-clock experience of living with something that many seek to deny.

SOME RESULTS

Perhaps it is not surprising that organizations involved with schizophrenia can confirm that its toll of misery is in no way decreasing. There is continuing news of one tragedy after another and these cases tend to be variations on a theme, with sufferers and their families kept in ignorance about the illness and how to cope with it. Instead, they have been given to understand that what has happened to them is caused by faulty family relationships and/or an inability or unwillingness of the patient to break away and live a 'normal' life. Families frequently report the spasmodic intervention of professionals who advise their sick relative to leave home and to live independently, but who seemingly make little effort to support the sufferer in this attempt at independent living. Relatives then find themselves in a 'double bind' where they cannot win; they either stand by and watch their loved ones falter and fall by the wayside, or they offer help and are accused of interfering (and apparently confirming their guilty role in their own dilemma!). Little account is taken of the fact that while professionals come and go, it is these same relatives who stay the course, picking up the pieces and accumulating a great deal of expertise along the way.

Similarly, when families eventually discover what is wrong with a very damaged relative, they may find that professionals will not cooperate with them in supporting the sufferer. One well-documented case[22] is that of the daughter of a London solicitor and his wife, whose illness started abruptly ten years ago when she was seventeen years of age. Since then Lorraine has received an assortment of 'labels' along the way, sometimes denied treatment both from GPs and hospitals when help has been sought, and at other times being hospitalized for long periods, sometimes with a diagnosis of schizophrenia and sometimes not. Occasionally she is aggressive, especially towards her mother with whom she has developed the clinging 'love–hate' relationship so characteristic of this illness. More often she is distraught.

One night in February 1988, her parents found her 'incoherent, afraid and half-naked, surrounded by two holdalls and some refuse bags containing all her possessions'.[23] She had been taken by social workers, without the parents' knowledge, to 'bed and breakfast' accommodation in a North London borough from an unsuccessful three-day stay in a mental health hostel. Previously she had a long placement in a therapeutic community. Her parents had been required initially to attend regular therapy sessions at the community, but otherwise to keep away and not make contact with Lorraine. They were seen by the staff there as the cause of her problem, having wanted, they suggested, to keep her as a sick, dependent child, using her as a scapegoat for their own sense of failure. Lorraine had been allowed to discontinue taking her medication and her contraceptive pills while at the community.

The young woman whom the social workers left with an Asian caretaker with little English and with no real knowledge about her, was *seven months pregnant*. Even at this stage, the Social Services department had not involved the parents in their 'plans'. It seems that the social workers accepted the therapeutic community's verdict on Lorraine's parents and anyway regarded Lorraine as their client, and one whom they considered to be capable of making rational decisions. It seems that this department does not talk of 'mental illness', only of 'special needs'. When Lorraine's parents found their destitute daughter, she was admitted to a teaching hospital, with a diagnosis of schizophrenia and described by the admitting psychiatrist as 'a very sick girl'. She was detained in the same hospital under a six-month order. She is still there over two years later . . .

Lorraine's case reveals an unquestioning and misplaced faith in the various ideologies of the 1960s which resulted in this vulnerable girl finally having none of the protections that many members of our society imagine it provides for any sick young person. There was no proper supervision of medication and contraceptive measures for someone very much at risk, no proper antenatal care, and she was eventually left in 'bed and breakfast' accommodation, where those in charge were unaware of, and had no understanding of, her 'special needs'. Is this the sort of service we expect our caring professions to provide?

Against the odds, Lorraine has survived this and other crises and she has found a safe harbour for a while, but for how long? Families with schizophrenia have to concentrate on one day at a time;

tomorrow may be an unknown minefield. It would be reassuring to believe that Lorraine's case is an exceptional one. Her family know it is not, and that is why they have become active members of the National Schizophrenia Fellowship and SANE (Schizophrenia: A National Emergency – an organization concerned with sponsoring research and raising awareness of the problems experienced by sufferers and their families), fighting to change attitudes and muddled thinking about this illness. Meanwhile the despair continues and *'normalization'* is the order of the day.

7 · Down a Slippery Slope

Freedom to be insane is an illusory freedom, a cruel hoax perpetuated on those who cannot think clearly by those who will not think clearly.

E. Fuller Torrey, MD, in *Nowhere to Go*, Harper and Row, 1988

So speaks a leading psychiatrist in the United States, a country further along the road to 'normalization' than we are and a country in which Edward Koch, then Mayor of New York City, pleaded for the destitute mentally ill on his streets:

If they can't care for themselves, shouldn't we help them? We wouldn't let five-year-old children live out on the streets and fend for themselves . . . both morally and legally we have an obligation to help those who can't or won't help themselves.[1]

At the end of the 1980s, we can see the consequences across the Western world of the spread of 'normalization' and the denial of serious mental illness. On the other side of the Atlantic, for example, both the psychoanalytical lobby and the anti-psychiatry movement have been more influential than in the UK. The move away from a medical model of mental illness in the United States was so pronounced that for many years psychiatrists interested in biomedical research found it difficult to get professorships.[2] In the late 1960s, the word 'deinstitutionalization' became a catchword in the United States and the discharge of long-term patients escalated into a chaotic disgorging from the hospitals of hundreds of thousands of individuals ill-prepared and ill-equipped for survival in the community. By the summer of 1981, an editorial in the *New York Times* commented: 'Deinstitutionalization has become a cruel embarrassment, a reform gone terribly wrong, threatening not only the formal mental inmates but also the quality of life for all New Yorkers.'[3] It has been estimated that New York City has around

36,000 homeless people living on its streets, and in 1980 a survey revealed that 60 per cent of these were moderately or severely mentally ill, with 7 per cent in need of psychiatric hospitalization.[4] These neglected and often overtly psychotic individuals have become human prey for the thug element in society and victims of thefts, savage beatings and rape. For example, a newspaper article commented at the end of a report on the beating to death of a homeless man and woman: 'The street people, among the most helpless of adult human beings, are the natural prey of anyone looking for some loose change, a pack of cigarettes, a bottle. They are rabbits forced to live in company with dogs.'[5]

The plight of untreated mentally ill individuals on city streets all over the United States is evident for all to see, and at last warning bells are beginning to sound in other countries which are themselves committed to 'deinstitutionalization'. Truly enormous sums of money were spent in the United States to provide a system of 'community care' via a vast new network of Community Mental Health Centers (CMHCs). These were intended to provide continuing care for the seriously mentally ill as well as preventive care for 'well' individuals whose mental health might be at risk. However, by the mid-1970s it was becoming clear that only a small proportion of those seen at CMHCs were schizophrenic, and by 1979 the President of the American Psychiatric Association reported:

Many programmes are moving from treating the most seriously and chronically mentally ill to providing care more oriented to social services – that is, care for patients with less serious illnesses and also assistance with their housing and sociocultural problems.[6]

Thus services set up in the community to replace those provided in the hospitals, have focused on a previously unacknowledged 'worried well' population, at the expense of the mentally ill who have been left floundering without any of the resources they need. Many explanations have been offered for this ludicrous state of affairs, but one critic has little doubt about the reason for the failure of the costly CMHC programme. Fuller Torrey says:

this failed mostly because there is no status in American psychiatry in providing care for schizophrenic patients . . . [they] are viewed as dull and uninteresting, needing only a prescription refill, and undesirable for the milieu of the waiting room because of their peculiar habits. The schizo-phrenic patients and their families got the message; they were not wanted.[7]

Although Fuller Torrey has also pinpointed other factors that have played, for him, a lesser part in this dismal failure in community care, we should consider carefully his comments on this phenom-enon of professional avoidance of the seriously ill. Back here in Britain, Edwina Currie, previously Junior Health Minister with special responsibilities for the mentally ill, observed towards the end of the 1980s: 'Professionals working with mentally ill people tend to concentrate on mild illness, as opposed to severe illness, as more people move from institutions into the community. Ministers are very conscious of this problem.'[8] Indeed, Peter Walker, the Secretary of State for Wales, warned during 1989: 'Experience elsewhere suggests that local services have often failed to make appropriate provision for those with more serious forms of mental illness, who are the most vulnerable.'[9]

Meanwhile, the lack of appropriate resources for the chronically mentally ill in the United States has been matched by the difficulty in obtaining urgently needed treatment for individuals suffering a psychotic breakdown. Civil liberties activists and organizations such as the American Civil Liberties Union (ACLU), which is closely linked to the American Bar Association, have contributed to a situation where protracted and complicated legal procedures can often render futile any attempts to admit a patient formally for urgent treatment. Kathleen Jones suggests that the ACLU publi-cation, The Rights of Mental Patients, presents a view of mental illness which virtually denies the existence of the condition. She describes the handbook as an exercise in advocacy, 'less in the interest of mentally ill people than in the interest of the legal profession, for whom the issues covered have provided many long and contentious legal cases, and much lucrative employment'.[10] The work of such bodies on both sides of the Atlantic does not rest with escalating the difficulties to be faced when trying to use the law to obtain urgently needed treatment for the mentally ill, it also has a profound effect on some of those sufferers who have the most to gain from medical treatment. The ridiculing of psychiatry together with exaggerated claims for both the dangerous potential of drugs and the beneficial effects of refusing treatment can be very attractive to victims of an illness based on paranoia.

The background to the tragic folly being played out across the Atlantic is carefully documented in the book *Nowhere to Go*, quoted at the beginning of this chapter, which is a searing indictment of the plight of the mentally ill in the United States. That rich country's ambitious mental health programme has become a timely warning for others to heed, and heed well before it is too late.

Meanwhile, what has been happening in Italy, the country that became a sort of 'promised land' for members of the anti-psychiatrist movement? It was in Italy that the movement had its major triumph, when Franco Basaglia, the charismatic, left-wing psychiatrist who became head of the mental health services in Trieste, originated a series of radical reforms, at a time of political turmoil. A fervent ideologist, he was also a gifted manager of men, and he used every means to hand, including enlisting the support of trade union and student movements, to oppose the existing mental health legislation and to introduce the community care system he envisaged. In time he had strong support in the National Assembly, and his movement, Psichiatria Democratica, eventually had enough public support to challenge the government of the day to bring in new mental health legislation on the lines that he was advocating. In 1978, under threat of a national referendum on the existing mental health law, which if successful could have left Italy with no mental health legislation at all, the government gave way.

Law 180, as it is known, banned the admission to hospital of any new patients other than on a forty-eight hour order and allowed for the emptying of the large old mental hospitals. Its emphasis was on 'normalization', and beds in the old mental hospitals were to be replaced by small fifteen-bedded crisis units to be set up in general hospitals for these short admissions, which could not be extended for a further seven days without the approval of a judge or mayor. These were to be known as 'diagnosis and cure' units, and the idea was that forty-eight hours would be enough time to sort out any social crisis and to refer the individual to the new psycho-social centres for treatment and support. It is not surprising to learn that in practice in many parts of Italy, these units are continuously 'blocked' with deeply disturbed individuals who cannot be cured in forty-eight hours, and the paperwork is 'rubber-stamped' by the appropriate local dignitaries. That, however, is not the case in Trieste, where the whole movement originated. After Law 180 was passed, Basaglia left to take on the awesome task of trying to sort out the mental health services in Rome. He died suddenly two years later, but it seems that his dream lives on in Trieste and most observers have been impressed by what they see there. Informal day resources, known as psycho-social centres, are staffed by psychiatrists and nurses and other mental health disciplines and volunteers. Clients come and go as they please, and have access to expertise as and when they want it. Some choose to spend a lot of their time at the centres, others are supported in their preference to stay at home, where untrained but enthusiastic staff visit them to help with domestic tasks. The fact that Trieste's unusually small 'diagnosis and cure' unit is rarely full suggests that the system is working as well as its fervent supporters claim. Jones and Poletti[11] were enthusiastic about what had been achieved in Trieste, but they found that several significant groups of people were not catered for by its services. For example, adolescents are excluded as they are seen to be the responsibility of their families (despite the fact that they are also, of course, the age group which is ripe for developing a schizophrenic illness), and so are the over sixty-five-year-olds (where there is an especially large contingent of such individuals, some of whom will develop the mental disorders connected with growing old). These writers have pointed out that although the official figures state that there are still 35,000 patients in mental hospitals throughout Italy, there is some confusion about the accuracy of this statistic because the hospital at Trieste and many others throughout Italy also accommodate what are known as 'guests'. In parts of Italy, Jones and Poletti have found 'guests' residing in locked wards, in strait-jackets or arm-muffs, and one strapped to his bed at his wrists and ankles.[12] Jones comments: 'the conditions in some Italian hospitals in the south must be among the most inadequate to be found anywhere in Western Europe. It is ironic that the reform movement should be claiming success when such conditions exist.'[13]

After a careful summary of what she has seen on her visits to Italy, Kathleen Jones suggests that the hotly debated 'Italian

Experience' is a misnomer for what should be called the 'Trieste Experience'. A well-defined and compact area bounded by mountains and sea, Trieste was ideally suited to Basaglia's dreams in that it was particularly manageable and had abundant available housing vacated by large numbers of Yugoslav workers. Neither criterion can be seen to apply to most of the rest of the country! Although Trieste and one or two other isolated areas have seemingly made Law 180 work, in Italy as a whole the reform movement's momentum is gradually running out, with all parties except for the Communists poised to introduce new legislation allowing more opportunity for admission for treatment of psychotic individuals and with facilities for longer-term hospitalization. Meanwhile, the old institutions, which had, it seems, a deservedly poor reputation before the new laws, are now even more neglected and run-down. Qualified staff are at a premium and the training of psychiatric nurses ceased in 1975. The outlook is not a rosy one; sought-after changes in legislation are not likely to be effected speedily and the government of the day has warned there is little money for public spending.

Meanwhile, what has been happening in the United Kingdom? At the end of 1988, Edwina Currie warned that we must avoid at all costs the situation that had arisen in some American cities where the most severely mentally ill people were discharged from hospital and left on the streets.[14] However, many observers point out that something very similar is already happening here. Back in 1985, the House of Commons Social Services committee reported: 'Large numbers are sleeping rough in archways and under railway bridges, some within hailing distance of the Palace of Westminster – hundreds, if not thousands, of mentally ill people without homes, or care of any kind'[15] and Malcolm Weller, a psychiatrist who practises in North London, has commented:

I started to talk to some of these people in the streets. I found almost all of them had fallen out of any kind of mental care. The new policies have created a large group of mentally ill people who are also physically ill, scraping out dustbins and sleeping on park benches.[16]

The charity Crisis at Christmas, which offers food and shelter for the homeless in London over the festive season, has voiced its concern regularly over the past few winters. Workers complain that there is inadequate provision for the aftercare of mental patients released into the community and some of their sick clients have been found to be actively psychotic.[17,18] St Mungo's, a charitable housing association which offers nightly shelter to homeless single young men in London, has seen a 500 per cent increase in the number of mentally ill using their services since 1983.[19]

Roger Harris, Chairman of the Association of London Authorities' (ALA) health panel, commented recently that all London boroughs are attempting to provide care for people who should properly be in a hospital setting. The ALA has produced a report on London's National Health Service which claims: 'The myth of community care conceals a grim reality – the toll of human casualties consigned to the tender mercies of bed and breakfast hostels, many people sleeping rough, others serving short sentences in police or prison cells.'[20] Perhaps all this was only too predictable if we consider the Audit Commission's finding in 1986 that

there are over 25,000 fewer hospital beds than there were ten years ago, but community facilities have not kept pace, with only an additional 9,000 day care places, for example; and no one knows what happens to many people after they are discharged.[21]

The signs of neglect are by no means confined to London. Some seaside towns have been a first choice both for mental health workers seeking 'bed and breakfast' accommodation for long-term patients without families to support them and for sufferers who have already slipped through the net and who have been attracted to these resorts. Some are relatively 'fortunate' and find accommodation which offers an adequate degree of human comforts, including caring or, at least, tolerance. All too often, others are ready prey for more unscrupulous landladies or landlords who are happy to cash in on a system that uses tax-payers' money to pay them handsomely for housing the mentally ill. Many chronically ill individuals persevere with quite horrendous living conditions and others are thrown out when their untreated symptoms become a nuisance. In March 1989, a disturbing article in the *Independent* Magazine described a 'schizophrenic drift' to the south coast, which the author found to be particularly pronounced in Hastings. Here the local people had reacted by resisting every attempt by charities to provide facilities for a growing population of outcasts, 'even down to a temporary winter night shelter'.[22] A recent official report on mental health care in the town has claimed that 'the local psychiatric outpatient services are inaccessible and [they] neglect the long-term chronically ill in favour of the "worried well" '.[23] Meanwhile, some of the homeless in Hastings are living *in caves* and one old lady was discovered after a couple of months, living in a railway toilet with the water in the lavatory pan beneath her frozen solid . . .

THE PENAL SYSTEM

Prison has been mentioned several times in this and previous chapters and it is now generally acknowledged that this has become one of the current alternatives to care for the mentally ill. This phenomenon would seem to be a direct result of two factors in the current approach to mental illness; the closure of the hospitals without adequate alternative provision and the requirements of latter-day mental health legislation.

It concerns, in the main, chronically ill men who are desperate to get someone to take care of them. A study of mentally abnormal men remanded to Winchester Prison[24] has revealed that when the courts have tried to refer such men for hospital treatment:

On a conservative estimate, one in five prisoners on remand were rejected for treatment. These generally were the men most in need of care and exhibiting the severest degree of social impairment. The majority of those rejected were suffering from schizophrenia.[25]

Where the men were on remand for criminal damage, a strong pattern emerged of:

a chronic schizophrenic perhaps discharged not that long ago from a mental hospital, but this time developing symptoms because he is no longer taking his medication, [becoming] destitute, too psychotic to get himself down to get his dole, throws a brick through a plate glass window of a shop and then waits for the police to arrive . . . The overwhelming proportion were petty and frequently offences to obtain food or shelter.[26]

Jeremy Coid, the forensic psychiatrist who conducted the survey, has suggested that a label of 'personality disorder' is being used as 'an excuse not to offer treatment'.[27] The Mental Health Act 1983 allows for the formal admission of individuals with a 'personality disorder' *which is treatable*. This, of course, is a label that many schizophrenia sufferers receive at least once during their career as a psychiatric patient. If a doctor chooses to concentrate on the difficult behaviour of a very psychotic individual, rather than on an illness which is causing that behaviour and which is urgently requiring drug treatment, this can provide an excuse for refusing admission to a sufferer who may be very unwelcome, because of shortage of available ward staff and beds, or because the hospital of referral likes to work with more rewarding patients. Although the psychiatrist who might be prepared to define 'personality disorder' in writing has so far proved elusive, there is probably general agreement amongst people who work with the mentally ill that we are talking in this instance about the type of personality that defies all attempts at treatment or help and creates mayhem within a community of any type, particularly a hospital ward.

However, it has been observed in the survey above that many of the individuals recommended by the courts for psychiatric treatment, who are refused admission to hospital on the basis of this label, have nevertheless improved with neuroleptic drug treatment. In other words, they have a treatable schizophrenic illness. It seems that we have here an example of some professionals in institutions *selecting out* the really vulnerable chronically ill sufferer in a similar way to some of their colleagues in the community.

There is a more sinister aspect to the rising numbers of the mentally ill who are falling foul of the law. Whereas all the studies of arrest rates and violent acts by mentally ill persons up until the middle of the century showed lower rates than those in the general population, Fuller Torrey points out that this is no longer the case in the USA since deinstitutionalization got under way. At least eight surveys since 1965 have found the rates for arrests to be considerably higher than for the general population, with a greatly increased likelihood of violence.[28] Similar findings are reported in Britain,[29,30] particularly among the homeless. This is another disturbing example of the effects of a 'normalization' approach and one which will, of course, do little to enamour society towards the cause of the mentally ill.

Meanwhile, a particularly worrying example of what can go wrong if a seriously ill person is put into prison rather than hospital is demonstrated in the case of Keith Hicks, who died in Brixton Prison hospital in 1985.[31] Aged thirty-eight at this time, he had suffered from epilepsy since the age of seventeen and from paranoid schizophrenia for about ten years; the latter was diagnosed when he attacked his mother in 1975. Supported throughout by his family and by a MIND day centre for the last three years before his death, where he was known by the staff as 'a gentle and very likeable person', Keith remained quite well until one night in October 1984 when he stabbed his father with a kitchen knife. The family had to get help from the police to restrain him and he was taken to Brixton Prison on remand. Although his family did not want him to be in prison and appreciated that a flare-up of his paranoid illness had been responsible for the attack, they were helpless to do anything about it at this stage. After two months in prison, Keith was admitted to King's College Hospital in a coma; seven days later he was back in Brixton. His trial was delayed because of his illness but on 1 March the court ordered that he should be detained in a psychiatric hospital under provision of the Mental Health Act and a bed was offered in Claybury Hospital where he had been treated previously. However, before the transfer could take place, his mother was turned away when she came to visit him and from 6 to 10 March she was told nothing other than 'He's not well.' Now very worried, on 11 March Keith's mother waited in vain for a call from the prison doctor. The next morning, a policeman came to tell her that Keith was dead.

No one from the prison made contact with Keith's parents and after the inquest they were no wiser as to what had happened. They sought help from MIND who appealed to the High Court to quash the verdict of misadventure given at the inquest. At a new inquest two years later, the family finally found out what had happened to Keith. According to evidence, during the last week of his life he missed twelve of eighteen doses of prescribed medicine and he suffered severe fits on 8 and 9 March. On 8 March a doctor recommended that he should be removed to hospital immediately.

From that time until his death on 12 March, Keith was not seen by a prison doctor although nursing reports recorded him as 'comatose stuporous, lying on the floor of his cell, incontinent of urine and faeces'.

The jury returned a unanimous verdict that his death was due to 'natural causes, aggravated by lack of care'. Lydia Sinclair, the legal officer of MIND, points out that there is no legal aid available for the representation of families at inquests such as the one held after Keith's death, and that the conduct of that inquest was thoroughly reviewed by the High Court and rightly criticized. Even more importantly, she argues that there is 'an urgent need for reform of a system which allows mentally ill people to be detained in prison rather than hospital and to be deprived of appropriate medical care'.[32]

COMMUNITY CARE?

In most parts of the United States it is now necessary to prove that the mentally ill individual is a danger to himself or to others before he or she can be formally admitted to hospital. One example of the law working in this way is described in *Nowhere to Go*. A man in jail in Wisconsin was said to be refusing all food and eating faeces. A doctor agreed that eating of faecal material on one occasion would not necessarily harm someone and the judge ruled the man was not a danger to himself and released him.[33]

Although the legislation in England and Wales does allow for admission 'in the interests of his health' as well as on grounds of safety, as previously mentioned, this is not appreciated by many of those working with the Mental Health Act 1983. Even where there *are* clear signs of danger to the sick person or to others, this may still not provoke action in some of the professionals concerned. In 1984, a Bexley hospital social worker was killed, with thirty-nine knife stabs, by a young woman who had previously been her client. Although the latter had apparently made several telephone calls to a psychiatrist threatening the social worker's life, and had tried to attack someone with a knife two months previously, none of the agencies involved with her had acknowledged just how ill Sharon Campbell was and just how urgent was her need for help and hospitalization. There were ample warning signs, so what is going wrong?

At one point in 1988, Chris Heginbotham, then director of MIND, acknowledged reluctantly that 'a number of psychiatrists aren't using some of the powers that they have under the 1983 Act'.[34] *But, why aren't they?* Anthony Clare sums up the concern of many critics of the existing legislation:

While there are several admirable controls built into the 1983 Act to ensure that patients are not detained wrongly and have access to an independent appeals tribunal, there are no equivalent controls to ensure that when they are suffering deterioration they are actually detained and treated.[35]

Not only do we have 'no equivalent controls' of this nature, but it is becoming increasingly clear that soon we may even run out of the sort of resources that are needed if sick patients are to be 'detained and treated'. On 20 November 1989, a television documentary[36] featured the Torbay area in the West of England, which had been singled out earlier by the Department of Health as providing an exemplary model of community care. It turned out that during recent months fourteen people had committed suicide on their discharge from hospital, and the Devon coroner had called for a halt to hospital closures until community care was improved.

In Torbay, the acute psychiatric services are mainly centred in a small modern hospital unit which caters for short admissions for acute bouts of psychosis as well as other types of mental illness. Relatives interviewed on the programme complained that the deceased had been discharged before they were well enough to cope in the community again. The brother of a woman now committed to Broadmoor Hospital for stabbing her mother to death, reported that the latter had taken notes which she had found in her home to the hospital staff and which seemed to indicate that her daughter was threatening to harm her. Nevertheless, the patient was sent home on leave at weekends and then discharged despite her mother's fears. Clearly, neither woman's interests had been served. As a result of the coroner's protest, the work of the Edith Morgan Unit was about to become the subject of a special enquiry.

Bearing in mind that the Torbay model has been widely cited and accepted as a desirable model for 'community care', it could perhaps be argued that we are a very long way off understanding even the basic requirements if those with a serious mental illness are to survive in the community. This is a sobering thought as we wait, poised, to lose the rest of our hospitals; the only available alternatives. Meanwhile, for some families it seems that asylum has already become a myth rather than a reality. Emma, a middle-aged woman who lives in the Midlands, became very ill after her mother's death, complaining she was being poisoned and that the police were after her. Early in 1989, fourteen long months after the family had first sought help for her, one of her sisters wrote to me:

After many months of pleading with the doctor and Social Services department, Emma was taken under Section 3 (a six-month order) to hospital where we thought she would be taken care of, but to our dismay we had a phone call to say she was missing. She was away for five days and returned home in a terrible state and was taken back to hospital only to go missing again a month later. This time she was missing for twenty-seven days with no word from her at all, again returning in a dirty state. She was taken back to hospital and went missing again two days later and this time the hospital discharged her! She eventually returned home in just the same state as when she went into hospital, but her GP said she was fit for work. Emma went back to work and again caused chaos in the office and was suspended, wandering the streets at night and staying in different hotels. She was afraid to stay at home because she believed people were breaking in; we begged and begged Social Services to do something but nothing happened. Then she began pestering a local Councillor to sack everyone in her office and he complained to Social Services who then took her in again under Section 3. This time they seem to be looking after her in hospital where she has stayed for over a month now.

Sadly, Emma went missing a few days later. Her psychiatrist does not believe she should be locked up, so Emma is never in one place long enough to be treated. She is admitted to hospital when her behaviour inconveniences other people in the community, particularly influential people. Her needs and her relatives' needs are seemingly irrelevant. Patients are admitted to hospital on section more often than not because they may be a danger to themselves or to others, yet it seems that there is less pressure on supervising medical teams and hospital managers to protect these individuals from themselves while they are sick than to protect their freedom. Those of her family who have not already given up on Emma are incredulous at the seeming lack of compassion and accountability of those to whom they turn for assistance. They feel that others should hear of their helplessness. I agree.

Emma's story is a very different one to Edward's. He also needed asylum and took his own life when he could not obtain this. His story was told on a BBC television programme[37] in the summer of 1988.

A gentle, sensitive young man, Edward's illness started abruptly in 1985 at the age of nineteen when he became aggressive and violent towards his mother one evening, holding her captive for several hours. As time went on, the situation worsened; his mother could get no help for her son or herself and he became withdrawn and increasingly deluded. Every so often he would erupt into violence again and she was forced to flee from her home more than once. At one point, he indicated to her that he thought he had schizophrenia. The psychiatrist at the local hospital said he could do nothing because Edward did not seem to want his help and did not turn up for out-patient appointments. However, many long months later, in the spring of 1988, Edward did seek help from the same psychiatrist; he asked to be detained under a compulsory order because he knew he would walk out of hospital otherwise. His request was refused and he was admitted on a voluntary basis. He discharged himself two days later. This scenario was enacted again the following week. He then drove to London and begged to be compulsorily detained in a hospital there, again to no avail. Later, back home, he asked a woman police constable who had known him since he was a child if she could get him detained in hospital, saying otherwise he was sure he would end up killing himself or someone else. She was shocked by his appearance and his obvious distress and again he was admitted to hospital, once more on a voluntary basis. A week or so later, he attempted to kill himself. Various members of Edward's family contacted the hospital, as they realized, like the policewoman, that he was now desperately in need of help. One night, he refused to return to the hospital after a visit to his mother. Apparently, hospital staff declined to listen to her protests. The next morning Edward was found in his car, dead from carbon monoxide poisoning.

Continual pleas for help over several years from an intelligent and sometimes terrorized mother were ignored. Early on, she was told that nothing could be done because Edward did not personally seek help. But when he was desperate enough to do this and to explain clearly how he could be helped, *he was not heeded*. A classic 'no win' situation?

Interestingly, it is not at all unusual to hear some recovered sufferers comment that they would not have been helped by admission to hospital during a past breakdown unless they had been sectioned because they needed to know that they could be returned there if they walked out. This is a measure of the potential innate restlessness of an acute psychosis and the almost compelling need to move on, anywhere! When well, such individuals have no doubt that survival for them at these times depends on firm and responsible action by others.

SUMMING UP

The past three chapters have looked into the background of all the muddled thinking that surrounds this illness and at some of the pitiable results of such ideas. Kathleen Jones has recently suggested that 'when the cobwebs of 1960s' thinking have been finally swept away the time may come for another step forward. For the truth is that we all have a long way to go.'[38] It is the aim of this book that we should take that step forward and preferably without further delay. We owe this to all the young people in the early stages of a schizophrenic illness. We have seen that those sufferers who become permanently and severely damaged may be rejected by both the health services originally intended for them and by the community in which they are expected somehow to survive. This being so, we must surely be morally responsible for protecting others from suffering this fate. If we can finally resolve to brush away those 'cobwebs', then perhaps we can find the courage openly to acknowledge this illness and our ability to do something about it.

8 · Back to Medicine

During the heyday of the anti-psychiatry movement, an Australian woman was asked by her doctor why she was so continually anxious and distressed. She shrugged her shoulders, replying, 'Well, you see, my son has this non-existent illness that won't go away . . .' What evidence do we have that schizophrenia does indeed exist and is not, as we know one cynic suggests, 'an endless list of broken social norms'?[1]

INCIDENCE

It has been realized for a long time that the incidence of schizophrenia is fairly constant at 1 per cent of the general population throughout the world. More recently, a World Health Organization survey started in 1977[2] revealed that the incidence of new cases of schizophrenia in ten countries was virtually identical, with about half of all cases having a serious outcome. The countries involved were Colombia, Czechoslovakia, Denmark, India, Ireland, Japan, Nigeria, the UK, the USA and the Soviet Union. Exactly the same criteria were used for the purposes of diagnosing the condition in individuals in all these very different cultures. Not only can this classic cluster of symptoms be identified in all these very different societies, but also in a similar proportion per population.

GENES

As we noted earlier, schizophrenia can – and does – run in families. Whereas most of the population run a 1 per cent risk of contracting the illness, this increases if you have someone in your family who is a sufferer. Generally, the risk for anyone with a blood relative who is a sufferer is as follows:

(1) An uncle, aunt, niece or first cousin; 2-3 per cent
(2) One parent, a non-identical twin, or other brother or sister; 10 per cent
(3) Two parents; 40 per cent
(4) An identical twin; 45 per cent

Another factor to bear in mind is the frequency and severity of the illness in the family, as this is also an indicator of the degree of risk. It is helpful also to remember that the chance of developing the illness decreases with age as so many first episodes of schizophrenia occur in young people between the ages of sixteen and twenty-five years.

These figures, gleaned from research throughout most of this century, are powerful evidence of a genetic component in this condition and have led Kety in the United States to comment wryly, 'If schizophrenia is a myth, it is a myth with a strong genetic component.'[3] However, the type of gene involved has eluded detection up until now. The hereditary factor is not at all straightforward and this may be demonstrated by another finding; that most schizophrenia sufferers are born to non-schizophrenic parents.

A genetic explanation of this illness was frowned upon for many years, partly due to memories of Naziism and partly due to determined efforts to prove that mental illness is a myth. The overwhelming evidence of the greatly increased risk for the second of a pair of identical twins (those that are formed from the same egg, thus sharing identical genes) if the first has schizophrenia, was submerged in continuous speculation as to why the second twin had a 50 per cent chance of *avoiding* the illness. This, it seemed, brought schizophrenia back into the province of the 'environmental' school of thought, and once more 'nurture' became more important than 'nature'. However, the continuing single-minded determination of such lobbies reaped one benefit because genetic research into this illness has of necessity become increasingly sophisticated during the post-war years. Studies which have supported a hereditary basis to schizophrenia date back to 1916. In

1938, Kallman reported on a study involving a very large sample of nearly 14,000 people[4] and revealed a significantly increased risk of the illness in first-degree relatives of sufferers.

TWIN STUDIES

In 1946, the same researcher reported his findings of a 65 per cent concordance rate for schizophrenia in identical twins, while for ordinary twins (who share half of their genes only, as do other siblings) this was only 8 per cent.[5] This latter figure was very similar to the apparent risks for ordinary brothers and sisters indicated in other studies. In 1953, Slater reported the results of his work in which he studied all admissions in London hospitals over a fourteen-year period, finding that identical twins had a concordance rate for schizophrenia that was around six times greater than that for non-identical twins.[6] Early twin studies found a concordance rate between 50 and 60 per cent, but these have been criticized for flaws in their methodology. Those in later years have found a lower rate of concordance, but the message has been consistent; twins who share exactly the same genes have a greatly increased rate of concordance for this illness compared with those who share just half of their genes like other brothers and sisters.

ADOPTION AND FOSTERING STUDIES

The continuous search for ways of separating environmental factors from hereditary ones resulted in long-term studies which followed up individuals who were born to schizophrenic mothers, separated at birth and brought up in other families. One such study in the 1960s found that five of fifty-seven such individuals became schizophrenic, whereas none of the control group of fifty children of non-schizophrenic mothers, similarly separated at birth, did so.[7] Similarly, a Danish study in 1972 looked at forty-four children who were born to schizophrenic sufferers, most of whom developed their illness some time after their illegitimate children had been placed in their adopted homes. Three of these were later diagnosed as schizophrenic, whereas not one of sixty-seven controls developed the illness.[8] In 1975, Kety and colleagues studied nearly

5,500 adoptions carried out in Copenhagen between 1924 and 1947, where the adoptive parents were not biologically related to the child.[9] Thirty-three of these children later became schizophrenic, and as a result of the researchers' careful assessment of these individuals' biological and adopted relatives and of those of the control group, Anthony Clare concludes:

This study strongly supports the view that genetic factors are of considerable importance in the transmission of schizophrenia. If family interaction patterns were of crucial aetiological importance, one would expect high rates of the illness in the adoptive relatives of schizophrenics, but those studies which have made a serious attempt to establish such a finding have notably failed to do so.[10]

DISCUSSION

Thus impressive work over many years, considerably helped by the remarkable population register kept by the Danes, has at last resulted in general agreement that not only does schizophrenia run in families but that where this happens it is highly probable that there is a strong genetic factor. Such is the rapidly growing confidence in this assumption that much of the scarce funding for research into this illness is currently focusing on a search for the offending gene or genes, with no fewer than twenty-eight teams currently involved in such work. Great excitement in the summer of 1987, when Gurling and his colleagues at Middlesex Hospital claimed they had identified such a gene,[11] soon died down when another team's work in no way replicated this finding. Research into this illness has always been bedevilled by the uncertainty as to whether schizophrenia is in fact a single entity or whether this classic cluster of symptoms represents the outcome of several different conditions. If the latter is true, then we may expect the search for the offending gene(s) to be beset with problems, but it may be that the results could eventually lead to the identifying of these different conditions or sub-groups.

There is growing evidence to suggest that it is between one-third and one-half of all cases of schizophrenia which run in families. Meanwhile, it seems increasingly probable that many of the remaining cases will turn out to be due to brain damage either around the time of birth, or perhaps earlier, in the foetus. It has been known for a long time that brain damage such as injury, tumours or temporal lobe epilepsy can lead to a condition with the characteristics of a schizophrenic illness, and several long-term studies and twin studies have led to a growing interest in the sort of complications during the mother's pregnancy and around the time of childbirth which can incur subtle brain damage. In 1988, Colin Blakemore commented that 'an old claim that many schizophrenics (more, at least, than among the general population) experience difficult births has recently been confirmed.'[12] What evidence do we have that such factors may be important?

The findings about identical twins excited interest in isolating environmental factors which might determine whether or not the second twin would develop this illness. Not surprisingly, the first clues about brain damage at birth came from researchers involved with twin studies. Back in 1967, Stabenau and Pollin reported their finding that where one identical twin had developed schizophrenia and the other had not, the affected one was more likely to have had a complicated birth.[13] Another twin study a few years later found that the one who developed schizophrenia was more often than not smaller at birth, had disturbed sleep and feeding patterns and certain bio-chemical and endocrinological changes.[14] In a rather different study in 1973, which compared individuals diagnosed as suffering from schizophrenia or personality disorder with their siblings, Woerner and his colleagues found that the schizophrenia sufferers had experienced a greater number of pregnancy and birth complications.[15] In 1981, Mednick and his colleagues published the results of their major long-term research study on behalf of the World Health Organization and they commented:

The high risk group [that is, children of a schizophrenic parent] which had not suffered breakdown had fewer perinatal difficulties than did the low risk control group. This suggested to us that perhaps there is a special interaction between the genetic predisposition for schizophrenia and pregnancy and delivery complications. It was almost as if in order for a high-risk subject to fare well, he needed a complication-free pregnancy and delivery.[16]

What evidence do we have of damage or changes in the brains of people with this illness? In an earlier chapter, we looked at one clear function of the neuroleptic drugs: that they restrict the amount of the neurotransmitter, dopamine, available to the brain cells. For some time, the significance of this was not understood, but two studies have established that in some individuals with this illness there is an increased number of dopamine *receptors* on the cells in various parts of the brain. In other words, there are far more opportunities for the dopamine to enter these particular cells. This would indicate *structural alteration to the brain*, and both studies demonstrated this phenomenon in sufferers who had not been treated with neuroleptic drugs as well as in those who had, seemingly confirming that the abnormality was not a response to the restriction of the dopamine levels by the medication.[17]

Similarly, we now know that in some schizophrenia sufferers the ventricles (vessels or spaces in the brain through which fluids flow), are slightly enlarged,[18] indicating a loss of actual brain tissue. It seems that this abnormality is present from the start of the illness. Recent twin studies suggest that this sort of brain damage is associated with the type of schizophrenia that does not run in families. In 1982, Adrianne Reveley concluded that 'some common environmental factor, possibly perinatal damage, may have led to the increase in ventricular size in discordant pairs, with schizophrenia developing in the more severely affected twin'.[19] Two years later, she and her colleagues found that only twins without a family history of schizophrenia had the ventricular enlargement, and the affected twin had suffered a more traumatic birth than its partner.[20]

There is ample evidence of abnormalities in brain functioning as well as organic changes in this illness, and one example of this are the various types of abnormal eye movements found in some people with a schizophrenic illness. It seems that certain types of abnormality in eye movements are associated with other conditions such as Parkinson's disease and Huntington's chorea, and at the time of writing research is in progress which is exploring any particular abnormalities of this kind in schizophrenia sufferers.[21] Other examples of altered brain functioning are abnormal electrical impulses in many sufferers and abnormal electroencephalograms for approximately one-third, particularly where there is no family history. There are many other neurological, biochemical and endocrinological changes referred to in the literature on schizophrenia. Brenda Lintner recently commented:

Brain function can be profoundly altered by biochemical disturbances which can occur, for example, when there are changes in the secretion of thyroid hormone or in diabetes. The profound nature of the disturbance of mental functioning in schizophrenia, the intensity of delusions and hallucinations . . . the fact that many schizophrenic symptoms can be reproduced by certain drugs and the consistently reported lack of response to psychotherapeutic intervention are all in favour of an organic causation.[22]

There are other features in schizophrenia which come up again and again, such as seasonal births, the possible involvement of viral infection, and persistent claims for the success of a dietary approach. It might be a good idea to take a look at each of these in turn.

Seasonal births: Reports of a significantly high concentration of births during the winter months of individuals who develop schizophrenia have been researched and confirmed in many parts of the world; this phenomenon is remarkably consistent, but more so in the northern hemisphere than in the southern.[23,24,25] Most of these winter births tend to be during the months of January, February and March and there is much speculation as to why this should be so.

Virus theories: Although it is not that unusual for other 'disadvantaged' births to take place at this time of year, some researchers believe that these seasonal births could support suggestions that schizophrenia is perpetuated by a virus[26] which may be more prevalent in these winter months and particularly so in urban areas. Fuller Torrey believes that an infectious disease theory could fit the facts;[27] it could, he believes, account for the observed changes in brain structure and function and explain many other mysteries. Certainly, there is other evidence that points to virus theories having some credence. We noted in an earlier chapter that case histories of first episodes of schizophrenia often feature a recent virus such as influenza or glandular fever, and that there is evidence of 'outbreaks' of acute attacks of schizophrenia during and after world-wide epidemics of influenza and sleeping sickness earlier in the century. Furthermore, Colin Blakemore points out,

'There is a high incidence of asthma and immunological deficiency in schizophrenics, which . . . suggests that infection or immune defects might be involved'.[28]

On a similar note, it has been recognized for a long time that people with schizophrenia appear to be especially vulnerable to the TB virus and this is referred to frequently in the literature. For example, Slater and Roth pointed out in the mid-1970s:

Many chronic schizophrenics died of TB at the time when conditions in mental hospitals favoured infection. The frequency of pulmonary TB [in schizophrenia] which . . . was four or five times that of the general populations, decreased with more hygienic conditions, but was still twice or three times that of non-schizophrenic patients living in the same hospital.[29]

An eating disorder? One of the first changes that many families note in a relative developing a schizophrenic illness is a deterioration in eating habits, with a preoccupation for sweet and stodgy snacks and for endless cups of tea or coffee. Many sufferers persistently seek stimulants such as caffeine and a few of them seem content to settle for a continuous diet of tea or coffee and cigarettes if left to their own devices. This relentless pursuit of stimulants leads to the need for more of the same due to the 'let down' effect which follows shortly after each drink or cigarette. Similarly, a large group of sufferers turn to sweet and stodgy foods made up of refined carbohydrates such as white flour, white rice, sugar, chocolate and ice-cream. This sort of diet also escalates the fluctuation of the body's blood-sugar levels, affecting mood and anxiety levels and creating a desire for more of the same foods. Some of these individuals have a seemingly insatiable appetite and the more they eat of these sorts of food, the more any courtesies and niceties are forgotten in their need to satisfy their craving.

Sandra experienced this sort of eating disorder. This athletic young woman had an acute schizophrenic breakdown from which she recovered quickly. She was not given the diagnosis nor was she told of the need for persevering for some time at least with medication. Eighteen months later she had a second breakdown and became very ill indeed, never in fact reaching her old potential again. Leading up to this second breakdown and for several months after it, Sandra became obsessed with the sort of food we have been discussing. On the day she was admitted to hospital, following a very stressful few hours and a tearful parting with her family, she suddenly became concerned only with getting there before the other patients had finished all the cakes for tea. . . . One day, back at home, she described to me the anguish she still felt before each meal trying to persuade herself that she could sit down at the table and not *ravage* her food in front of her family as she knew this distressed them so much. She added that she never seemed to have any success with this. So desperate was her craving that she would jump up after her meal each evening and proceed to cook a whole tray of buns which she would then immediately devour on her own. Much later, with the return of rather better health, Sandra's appetite and tastes in food returned to normal.

Sandra's experience demonstrates the compelling nature of this addiction which is aggravated by eating the very foods that are craved, and which can frequently be observed among sufferers *whose schizophrenic symptoms are not properly controlled.* It is important to emphasize this, as many professionals assume that these abnormal eating habits are caused by the appetite-stimulating action of the neuroleptic drugs. Many families can confirm that this distorted craving for sweet, stodgy foods and stimulants can be observed in individuals developing a schizophrenic illness before any treatment begins and also in those who deteriorate after giving up medication. Similarly, there are sufferers who regularly take neuroleptic drugs who never show any signs of such eating disorders. I do believe that anybody with this illness who exhibits these sorts of eating habits should be encouraged to move away from these refined foods to a diet with more emphasis on fruits, vegetables and proteins. Interestingly, the influence of our modern junk foods on a schizophrenic illness may well be confirmed by the recent World Health Organization study's finding that the actual *course* of the illness tends to be more benign in some of the under-developed countries.[30]

Throughout this century there have been continuing claims that the consumption of certain cereals may have significance in a schizophrenic illness. Two American studies [31,32] have noted a raised incidence of coeliac disease in people who develop schizophrenia and in their relatives. Coeliac disease is a condition involving crippling diarrhoea, which can also provoke emotional disturbance and even psychotic-like behaviour. It is treated by the exclusion of gluten from the diet, and, in some cases, milk as well. An American psychiatrist called Dohan was impressed by the lowered level of first-time schizophrenia admissions to hospital in Europe during the Second World War, particularly in the occupied countries, and pointed out that this coincided with a dearth of wheat and similar cereals in these areas. Work in the late 1960s and 1970s supported the hypothesis that a diet excluding these foods can escalate the recovery from a schizophrenic breakdown in some individuals and that reintroducing them can exacerbate psychotic symptoms.[33,34] Research has since been carried out which demonstrates that wheat and milk proteins which are not broken down completely before entering the bloodstream can be traced to the brain.[35] Similarly, Zioudrou, Streaty and Klee[36] have demonstrated that opioid peptides are derived from wheat and milk proteins in the course of digestion and that these have similar properties to the naturally occurring molecules called endorphins, which affect the functioning of the brain, acting as hormones and neurotransmitters. These dietary peptides are called exorphins and exhibit a morphine-like activity. Dohan suggests that a fault in the permeability of the gut walls might allow food-derived neuro-active peptides to get into the brain cells.[37] Certainly, it is common to find gut and bowel disorders in sufferers and in their relatives and one team of British research workers reported in 1987 that:

the findings of this study are consistent with the hypothesis that a proportion of patients with chronic psychiatric illness, including schizophrenia, have abnormal small intestinal mucosal permeability, resulting in an increased absorption of endorphin-like molecules from the intestine.[38]

Such is the persistence of claims about wheat gluten that interest in this subject has revived recently. So far, attempts to replicate the earlier findings have failed, but this may well be because they have set out to prove, with inappropriately small sample populations, something which has never been claimed: that this sort of sensitivity applies *across the board* for people with schizophrenia.[39] My own observations throughout the 1980s have been that a diet excluding wheat and other gluten-containing cereals can have a remarkable effect for some sufferers, and especially, but not exclusively, for those exhibiting the sort of eating disorder discussed earlier. When it is effective, this measure seems to enhance the function of the neuroleptic drugs, bridging the gap between the controlling of symptoms and a dramatic recovery of former potential, particularly combating 'negative' symptoms such as lethargy and sleepiness during the day. Because the rewards for some can be so great, it would seem worthwhile for all sufferers to be encouraged to try this straightforward and harmless measure for a month or two. I really see no virtue in waiting until we understand better whether this type of food sensitivity can be a causative or contributory factor to a schizophrenic illness, or whether it exacerbates the condition once it is present. My first book, *Schizophrenia: A Fresh Approach*, discusses this subject in some detail, together with suggestions for menus and recipes.[40]

A MEDICAL ENTITY?

Clearly, there are several main themes which keep recurring in this search for a greater understanding of schizophrenia; genes, brain damage, risk factors around the time of birth, virus infections and the detrimental effect of some foods. No wonder that one team of researchers, involved in retrospective studies concerning genetic risk, time of the year and conditions of birth, have argued that their data suggest several different avenues by which an individual may come to be schizophrenic.[41] Several theories so nearly fit the facts without any of them providing the answers that are sought. This, of course, would be predictable if, as is now suspected, schizophrenia does represent several different disorders which all lead to the same cluster of symptoms. Certainly, we have no reason to join doubters such as Bentall, Jackson and Pilgrim (Pilgrim, as we have seen, condemns a genetic approach to schizophrenia because of the record of Naziism in the 1930s and 1940s) who say:

given that schizophrenia is an entity which seems to have no particular symptoms, which follows no particular course and which responds to no (or perhaps every) particular treatment, it is perhaps not surprising that aetiological research has so far failed to establish that it has any particular cause.[42]

It is perhaps difficult to comprehend that these authors are talking about the same conditions discussed in the 1970s by two well-known British psychiatrists:

The universal incidence of the disease in all races and cultures weighs heavily against any arguments that environmental and psychological factors of any specific kind play an important part in causing the disease; and so does the experience of the clinician who sees identical clinical pictures in patients from all walks of life and from the most diverse family and educational backgrounds.[43]

Increasingly, schizophrenia is being compared to conditions such as diabetes and Kety points out that:

Diabetes mellitus is analogous to schizophrenia in many ways. Both are symptom clusters or syndromes. . . . Each may have many aetiologies and shows a range of intensity from severe and debilitating to latent or borderline. There is also evidence that genetic and environmental influences operate in the development of both. The medical model seems to be quite as appropriate for the one as for the other.[44]

What, then, are the rationale and advantages of using such an approach? Quite simply, the use of the medical model implies that something is wrong which needs medical assessment and attention. If we develop a worrying symptom, most of us will approach our GP, hoping that this professional will reach a diagnosis by assessing the situation and recognizing our symptoms. Fifteen years ago, Slater and Roth pointed out:

When treatment was restricted to institutional care and occupation therapy, early diagnosis was scarcely important, but with the coming of the modern physical treatments and *the realization that the best results are obtained in early cases* [my italics], it has become of the first importance to recognize the illness at its beginnings.[45]

Indeed, we have plenty of evidence that the denying or delaying of a diagnosis of schizophrenia can be damaging to the sufferer. First, the sorts of experience described earlier, in Chapter 2, can lead to failure at college, to the end of long-held career plans, to the destroying of valued relationships and to loss of dignity and self-respect. At worst, deep despair, or the influence of auditory hallucinations can lead to death. Second, we know that each and every breakdown can bring with it the risk of the Type II syndrome, involving irreversible damage. Third, the Northwick Park Study researchers found evidence that susceptibility to later relapses correlates with initial delays in receiving drug treatment, suggesting that people who are diagnosed and treated quickly will have a better chance of making a real recovery.[46]

What, then, is stopping us from providing an effective service for people developing this illness? Why is it that we seem unable to achieve with schizophrenia a normal process of *assessment and recognition*, followed by *diagnosis and acknowledgment*?

ASSESSMENT AND RECOGNITION

Although GPs are the gateway to all the available mental health services, many of these key professionals have had very little opportunity to acquire any real knowledge of psychiatry. In 1981, the Acheson Report commented on GPs having little or no specific training in dealing with mental illness and a lack of awareness of other relevant services and resources,[47] and in 1988 a British Junior Health Minister stressed the importance of 'prevention' in mental illness and mentioned the possibility of 'finding ways of helping GPs identify and treat psychiatric problems at an early stage'.[48] Although younger GPs who have trained over recent years have received a little more relevant input, there is no doubt that there are doctors who are not aware of the early signs of a schizophrenic illness. At a conference that I attended recently, one courageous middle-aged practitioner asked the panel on the platform for a list of the early signs which he, as a GP, should look for. Sadly, none was forthcoming; just an embarrassed silence, followed by a change of subject. Even those doctors who would be aware of the warning signs may well be put off by lack of any immediate back-up support from the specialist services. Some idea of the scale of the problem with obtaining recognition and appropriate help for a sick relative can be gleaned from findings of a large survey carried out during the 1980s within the membership of the National Schizophrenia Fellowship; in 185 out of 889 first episodes, the GP was not prepared to treat the problem seriously and in another eighty cases, the GP was sympathetic but could not get help from the psychiatric services.[49]

In most instances the GP will be the first point of contact for sufferers and their families, and any move towards a preventive approach to schizophrenia would make it imperative that these professionals should have access to further training, including a checklist of the main pointers to look for in a developing schizophrenic illness and an information pack on the available appropriate local services and resources. It is equally important that they should receive adequate back-up support when they wish to refer a vulnerable patient for specialist assessment and treatment.

Meanwhile, the experiences of families all over the country and the findings of the Northwick Park Study of First Episodes[50] demonstrate that there can be repeated calls for help while the individual's behaviour becomes increasingly bizarre, and sometimes even dangerous, before the illness is acknowledged. Perhaps it would be worth taking a look at this enigma; why should it be so difficult to obtain a diagnosis of such a common illness?

A DIAGNOSIS

The need for an agreed and accepted set of criteria for diagnosing this illness has always been acknowledged. The lack of any such criteria would, of course, provide ammunition for cynics determined to deny its existence. Furthermore, the existing implications for any individual given this diagnosis make it desirable that it should be reached by as standardized an approach as possible. Equally, without such criteria there is no foundation from which to build up a meaningful fund of knowledge. For example, until recently the use of different sets of criteria in different countries made the results of research muddled and confusing. Although British studies back in 1959 and 1964[51,52] revealed that there was in fact a higher rate of agreement on diagnosis for schizophrenia than for other psychiatric conditions, Kendall reported in 1972 that reliability decreased if opinions were drawn from psychiatrists in different countries, pointing out that 'there are large and persistent differences in the usage of this term in different parts of the world'.[53]

More specifically, the World Health Organization's International Pilot Study of Schizophrenia in the early 1970s found that the criteria for diagnosing the illness in seven of the nine countries involved was fairly consistent, but was considerably broader in the other two: the USA and USSR.[54] In recent years, there has been much more worldwide agreement on the definition of schizophrenia, but attempts to make the criteria more uniform for research purposes tend inevitably to bring with them negative features such as narrower boundaries and less flexibility. It is now generally agreed which symptoms are required to be present for a diagnosis of schizophrenia to be considered; the difficulty here is not definition but recognition! However, the perceived necessity to impose certain conditions that must apply in order for the diagnosis to be valid may be more contentious. Perhaps a closer look at one of the diagnostic tools used widely during the 1980s, and in the United States in particular, might make this a little clearer.

The third edition of the *Diagnostic and Statistical Manual of Mental Disorders* (known as DSM III)[55] lists the sorts of symptom that are characteristic of a schizophrenic illness and specifies that at least one of these must be present at the time of diagnosis alongside certain other provisions. For example, one of these stipulates that recognized symptoms must have been present *for at least six months*. But why? Who exactly has been able to establish such a precise timing for the confirming of a schizophrenic illness or a method of measuring this? Why is schizophrenia more real after twenty-six weeks than before? What does such a requirement do to statistics based on the diagnosis on a first admission to hospital? Who is to determine whether symptoms have persisted for at least this period of time? I know sufferers who have realized when recovered that they were experiencing symptoms *long before they were aware of them as such* and, understandably, long before there were any outward signs of their illness.

Another condition is that there should be a deterioration in functioning in such areas as work skills, social relations and self-care. This is not quite so straightforward as it sounds and is only applicable if it is appreciated that it is quite possible for a deterioration to be observed in one of these – probably social relations (because of withdrawal) – while work skills and self-care may be unaffected. This is not always recognized, and an ability to function appropriately in the other two spheres can, and does, deceive.

A further condition requires that the illness appears before the individual's forty-fifth birthday. Is nature aware of such rules, and what is this illness if it comes along a few days/weeks/months later, and does this include the elusive six-month qualifying period discussed above? Such a condition seems to deny a previously accepted view that a small group of women sufferers develop the illness after their menopause – and they do!

Another condition is that the individual's symptoms are not suggestive of a manic depressive illness. The difficulties with such an innocuous-sounding requirement have been touched on in an earlier chapter. The symptoms of schizophrenia and a manic depressive illness can often overlap, and there are individuals who end up being given a 'midway' diagnosis of schizo-affective disorder, and others who are unfortunate enough to receive no diagnosis at all because of the difficulties involved!

All other diagnostic measures in this illness have contained similar pitfalls and problems in trying to establish beyond doubt that the presence of certain symptoms is indicative of a schizo-phrenic illness. To my mind they make the reaching of a diagnosis more rather than less hazardous and still leave the doctor with the problem of confirming the existence of specific symptoms – the really important factor when all is said and done. Bearing in mind the almost inevitable defensiveness of the patient, such an achieve-ment can demand real skills in observation, interviewing and listening. I mention 'listening' for two reasons; the first is that a real clue (sometimes intentional) from the sufferer can be, and often is, missed, and the second is that the most relevant sources of information – those closest to the individual – may not even be tapped. Even at this stage in the proceedings, these precious resources are still frequently ignored. The most prompt and accurate diagnosis tends to be the one made by the professional *who tunes in to the misery* of an otherwise well-defended sufferer and who listens carefully to what relatives have to say about the changes which have taken place. Sometimes there is little consideration given to such crucial matters, and I have known psychiatrists who depend entirely on their interviewing skills, ignoring relatives and involved professionals alike. One psychiatrist takes a very long time – sometimes over a year – to confirm the opinions of those closest to the patient, and when this eventually happens it is usually because of increasing evidence of sickness rather than because the doctor obtains precisely 'correct' answers to a checklist of questions.

For whatever reason, there is widespread tendency to miss or avoid diagnosing schizophrenia even when patients are ill enough to be admitted to hospital because of the havoc their illness is wreaking. Recent Danish research[56] demonstrated that only 50 per cent of all male sufferers and 40 per cent of all female sufferers first admitted to hospital in Denmark in 1972 were diagnosed as having schizophrenia at that time, although it is clear in retrospect that this illness was the reason for their admission to hospital. It may be that some doctors place too much emphasis on adhering carefully to recognized criteria, so necessary and valuable for the purposes of worldwide research and for statistics, but less so for individual sufferers urgently needing help. Certainly, others go to great lengths to avoid a stigmatizing 'label' for their patients. This hesitation or reluctance over diagnosing schizophrenia does not help patients to understand what is happening to them, nor to protect themselves from further damage. Furthermore, it can lead to possible complacency over the incidence of the illness[57] as many 'first-time admissions' for schizophrenia do not appear in the statistics as such; they feature under different diagnoses.

It is a pity that the inherent difficulties of separating out and defining the different psychoses should be escalated by the requirements of research that may itself be beleaguered by these same difficulties. As discussed earlier, in Chapter 3, work by the Northwick Park Hospital team suggests that conditions such as schizophrenia and manic depressive illness may be part of a continuum of conditions, all with certain symptoms in common that are responsive to the action of the neuroleptic drugs.[58] It is perhaps a sad irony that delay in diagnosing a schizophrenic illness usually results in the withholding of such medication. Let us take another look at the important role this can play in this type of illness.

APPROPRIATE DRUG TREATMENT

As we have seen, it was chance that finally made the neuroleptic drugs available to psychiatry, and decades later they remain the only effective tools available for this illness. Not only does neuroleptic medication quickly control, and often relieve, the symptoms of an acute schizophrenic illness, but it also greatly reduces the risk of further relapse. Nevertheless there are doctors, perhaps embarrassed by prevailing attitudes to the medical model, who seem to be unaware that the medical profession has at last inherited an effective weapon which, *when used promptly and with skill*, can very often stop most of the ravages of this illness. What is often overlooked is the vital importance of persevering with finding the right amount of the right drug for each patient. One well-recovered sufferer has commented:

A certain amount of experimentation must go on to find exactly the right formula of drugs for each patient. Trial and error can be painful, but it was worth it in my case. Now I have a complete drug regime to stabilize my mood and keep the imaginings at bay without in any way making me *feel* drugged.[59]

Just how skilled a judgement is involved in finding the right levels for each patient can be gleaned from the fact that over 100-fold variations of chlorpromazine blood levels between different patients on the same dose have been reported.[60] I know several sufferers who are leading absolutely normal lives, with the help of greater doses of neuroleptic drugs than some psychiatrists would dream of prescribing. Indeed, Fuller Torrey pleads for proper trials of different drugs for those who do not respond well to their medication. He argues that, contrary to public opinion, it is more common to find undermedicated rather than overmedicated schizophrenic patients.[61]

I can find no evidence to suggest that a larger dose of these drugs, which enables the individual *to function well*, is more dangerous than a lower one. We do know, however, that an uncontrolled psychosis is detrimental to the sufferer's health. Sadly, there is a growing trend for doctors to judge the effectiveness of their treatment by their success in continuously reducing the dosage of medication. This can result in potentially well sufferers losing a firm grip on reality and having a constant struggle of willpower to 'stay in there'. Too often, this leads to relapse and the prescription of *enormous amounts of the same or a similar drug* to bring them to the point where they can once again face the uphill struggle back to better health. What is the sense in this? The genuinely well schizophrenia sufferers are often the ones who are very sensitive to adjustment of these chemicals and who are encouraged to remain on the dosage that enables them *to function effectively*. Some doctors are happy for their recovered patients to keep a small supply of extra tablets available for times when they feel vulnerable. This arrangement works well for such individuals; having the opportunity to be partly in control of their medication (and, thus, their lives) can be both rewarding and reassuring. It makes good sense too; it is not widely recognized that it is a feature of this illness that the levels of medication frequently need minor adjustments for perhaps a few days at a time. This sort of arrangement should present no hazards; it is also a feature of this illness that sufferers are reluctant to recognize the need to take medication. When they are well enough to have insight into their illness, they can and do learn to recognize the first warning signs of returning symptoms. Those who are not well enough to distinguish clearly between reality and returning symptoms, almost invariably have to be persuaded to agree to an adjustment of medication.

All drugs bring with them danger; even the common aspirin is harmful for some individuals but has life-saving properties for others with heart disease. Although the drugs used in schizophrenia are safer than many others used in medicine, their dangers are constantly being emphasized. We do not hear of arthritis sufferers, for example, being exhorted to struggle on without medication, as happens in mental illness. Nor do we hear of their drugs being described as 'chemical strait-jackets', a popular phrase among civil rights lobbies, some academics, and, more worryingly, some mental health professionals. Why, I wonder, is it desirable to seek an antidote for physical disease and pain but not for a mental illness and all the torture that can result? The search is under way for medication that will continue to combat schizophrenic symptoms, but without the side-effects and possible dangers inherent in the existing drugs. Meanwhile, instead of shunning existing measures to relieve suffering in other people (and so reinforcing the inherent reluctance in those who need such treatment), perhaps we should put more emphasis on making sure that the progress of all those on medication is carefully monitored. This is by no means always the rule at the present time.

EMBRACING THE RIGHT SORT OF MEDICAL MODEL

I sometimes meet psychiatrists who greet me with the comment that their role is not an important one and that the rest of the multi-disciplinary team contribute more to the patient's recovery. I have found this to be bad news if they are speaking of schizophrenia. Quite simply, the rest of the team may have a great deal to offer only if the supervising doctor understands the vital role of medication in this illness and *first practises good medicine*, stabilizing patients on an acceptable drug regime and freeing them from a psychotic night-mare so that they are able to function properly again. The World Schizophrenia Fellowship has pointed out the recent trend in which 'professionals cross discipline boundaries and become "schizophrenia specialists", knowledgeable and helpful in many areas'.[62] This has to be an encouraging trend in an area shunned for so long, and a trend which may go a long way towards promoting the cause and meeting the needs of sufferers and of those who love them. Meanwhile, as one such specialist, I know only too well that the first priority in working with this illness is the skilled prescrib-ing of the appropriate medication which can only be legally carried out by the doctor supervising the patient's treatment. The with-holding of this, intentional or otherwise, might be seen as an awesome responsibility in our present state of knowledge. Each and every sufferer has the right to the benefit of skilled medical practice, together with the involvement of all the other appropriate skilled services which can contribute to the resumption of good health and a rewarding lifestyle. The next chapter will take a careful look at just how much can be achieved by everyone working with this illness.

9 · Another Way Forward

Years ago, the late John Pringle, OBE, wrote: 'Failures in coordination and communication seem to hang about the administrative management of schizophrenia almost like a grim parody of the condition itself.'[1] Little has changed since the founder of the National Schizophrenia Fellowship made this comment back in 1970; many sufferers and families seem fated to stumble again and again through a chaotic maze of muddle and non-communication. Those closest to someone developing a schizophrenic illness first have to cope with their own ignorance and with that of most of the rest of society. When they are eventually convinced that the individual is sick, they may then have to cope with a conspiracy of silence from professionals who frequently provide no explanations, let alone attention and treatment for the sufferer. Often patients are advised to encourage this particular offspring to 'leave the nest' at a time when this is most unwise. When they reluctantly do this, it is only to find later that no one accepts responsibility for keeping a watchful eye on the vulnerable young person. With the breakdown which usually follows these delaying tactics, the inevitable crisis may be prolonged by a GP maintaining that the patient must actively seek help before he or she can intervene. Even when this is acknowledged as impractical, the GP may or may not see an immediate need for a domiciliary visit from a psychiatrist. When such a service is provided, anxious relatives may be told that the patient is ill, but 'not sectionable' or that the patient should be in hospital but the doctor has no beds available at that time. Finally, the nearest relative may not be aware of his or her rights under the Mental Health Act 1983.

Amazingly, when a diagnosis is finally agreed and appropriate treatment is given, many families find themselves facing the same attitudes and obstacles all over again if their relative starts to relapse. Even where after-care is provided, this will be ineffective unless those responsible for the sufferer's medical supervision listen carefully to relatives or others close to the individual if they report signs of relapse. Too often, early calls for help are shrugged off during that vital period in which the sufferer would be prepared to accept help. The situation may be further aggravated by a psychiatrist intent on adhering to principles of medical confidentiality, thus sabotaging any remaining hope of sensible communication. Families report that they find themselves facing the same attitudes and obstacles all over again each time the sufferer starts to relapse. There is little evidence of learning by experience; the message seems to be that this is a hopeless condition and nothing will be gained or lost by taking prompt action. This laid-back 'let's wait and see' approach to this serious, but treatable, illness militates against any sensible preventive action. It occurs again and again. *Surely we can do better than this?* I believe we can, but only if we start thinking in terms of prevention and minimizing damage rather than of avoiding and denying what is happening.

ATTITUDES

At the start of the 1990s, a health minister commented that he shared the desire to bring the disease (schizophrenia) out into the open so that politicians, consultants and GPs would become aware of the scale of the problem.[2] Attitudes to this illness are reminiscent of attitudes to cancer fifty years ago. This was a word that was never mentioned in public, especially by the medical profession. Later, as it became associated with famous movie stars and other public idols who had the courage to talk about their illness, cancer became a household word magically divorced from its previous stigma. Nowadays, no one is ashamed to say they have had cancer and because of this we all know that there is life after such an illness! A lot of the fear of cancer has disappeared along with the stigma. The same will happen for schizophrenia when those sufferers who survive and get on with their lives no longer have to keep this secret. There are successful individuals, as well loved today as some of those who made cancer acceptable yesterday, who may feel able to say, 'I've had a schizophrenic breakdown.' However, this will not happen until health professionals come to terms with this illness and are able to acknowledge and discuss the diagnosis openly with such potentially well sufferers. What are we waiting for? With the advent of community care, we really cannot afford to wait any longer.

THE WAY FORWARD

A Member of Parliament recently told the House of Commons that 'The public needs to be educated about the fact that the illness [schizophrenia] can strike suddenly, without warning and in any family. A public that is educated will also be educated about ways to help.'[3] She is right. Let us start sharing this information with that section of the population most at risk; we should be talking to young teenagers and to parents'/teachers' associations in our schools, warning them of the specific dangers of experimenting with street drugs and telling them of the early signs of a developing schizophrenic illness. It has been my experience that young people show more aptitude than their elders for accepting a schizophrenic illness in a friend. They also show encouraging signs of wanting to learn about such matters. They certainly should each have the opportunity to make an *informed choice* about experimenting with soft drugs. We need to talk to church workers, to young wives' groups, to young mothers at clinics and to any club or organization that welcomes speakers, getting the message over in a matter-of-fact way which emphasizes the treatability of this very common condition and the preventive measures that can be taken. In particular, the media will have an important part to play in taking the ignorance, fear and stigma out of the word *schizophrenia*.

ACKNOWLEDGMENT

What do we know about this illness that sometimes seems to be the final taboo? Not a lot, perhaps, but we do know that we are talking about a classic cluster of symptoms which may have different origins and which can inflict varying degrees of handicap on those who experience them. For the purpose of understanding better how schizophrenia can influence the lives of those affected, we can divide sufferers into four groups:

(a) Around 25 per cent who have no more than one breakdown but who may continue to need medication and who may experience residual symptoms.

(b) Those who have intermittent breakdowns, either becoming reasonably well in between times or gradually deteriorating with each relapse.

(c) Those who suffer permanent damage, having 'negative type' symptoms with a detrimental change in personality and social functioning, as well as remaining at risk of further breakdown.

(d) Around 10 per cent who need ongoing intensive care and support, and who may suffer either or both types of symptom.

We do not have any other words at this time with which to differentiate between these very different groups of sufferers, nor can we separate out the experiences of each of them, because they overlap. Other illnesses have similar variations; polio, for example, can be experienced as a 'flu-like episode, as the loss of use of one limb or as total paralysis. Instead of avoiding the recognition of the proper diagnosis in the potentially well groups (a) and (b) above, which, of course, include many very attractive and able individuals in whom we may wish to deny any signs of schizophrenia, we would do them a far greater favour by acknowledging their vulnerability and helping them to stay well. Those in group (a) will stand little chance of any real quality of life if they are not given an explanation for what has happened to them and if they do not recognize any residual symptoms for what they are. Those in group (b) will be put at risk if they recover from a first breakdown without knowing they may be vulnerable to relapse; they have the right to know this and to learn how to protect themselves, particularly as further breakdowns can lead to the type of illness suffered by group (c). At present, many professionals do not acknowledge schizophrenia until they see the level of handicap experienced in groups (c) and (d); *this is too late for the potentially well sufferers in the other groups*. If we are to minimize the amount of wastage caused by this illness, then we must acknowledge it as soon as the tell-tale signs of its development are apparent. It is not enough to know about the symptoms of this illness; unless new sufferers seek help very early on when they can still trust others, they will not acknowledge or even understand what is happening to them. We then have to rely on *signs* that might indicate the presence of such symptoms; fortunately there are ample signs.

What are these pointers; what should lead to a suspicion of a diagnosis of schizophrenia? Chapter 2 looked at most of the features of this classic cluster of symptoms; what are likely to be the first signs of their presence? To simplify our task, we can divide them into three groups: (a) physical, (b) behaviourial and (c) anecdotal.

Physical
Sleep disturbance, especially turning night into day
Change of menstruation pattern in young women
Changed eating habits
Haggard features and haunted-looking stare in the eyes
Inability to make eye contact
Untypical and continuing complaints of all sorts of physical ailments

Behavioural
Withdrawal from favourite activities
Withdrawal from friends
Spending hours in own room, often accompanied by playing the same one or two records noisily for hours on end
Closing the curtains during daytime
Refusal to eat with others
Untypical avoidance of TV or radio
Lack of interest or pride in appearance and personal hygiene
Unexplained bouts of hostility
Bad language that is quite out of character
Clinging behaviour towards one person in a previously independent individual, while remaining detached

Anecdotal
Reports of unexplained unhappiness in the individual
Puzzled reports that *something is wrong*

Reports indicating a worrying change in personality for which there
is no obvious cause

If these sorts of feature are present, then the right questions
should elicit from the individual and the family whether or not
predictable symptoms are the underlying reason for them. If the
diagnosis is one of schizophrenia, then the sooner it is acknowledged, the sooner the recognized treatment can begin and the
better the prognosis is likely to be. If help is offered early enough to
individuals developing schizophrenic symptoms, then they will in
all probability be responsible and cooperative. As we have seen,
during the first stages of breakdown sufferers are aware that
something is very wrong, and they are frightened. There is a short
period during which they will trust others and listen to advice. An
explanation that a chemical imbalance can cause distorted
perception of the five senses and confuse the brain is probably all
that is needed initially, particularly if examples are then drawn from
the individual's own experience. A recommendation that a low
dosage of neuroleptic medication be prescribed to combat this
imbalance, together with an explanation of possible side-effects, is
quite likely to be acceptable at this stage if accompanied by the firm
suggestion that progress should be monitored frequently over the
first two or three weeks.

DIAGNOSIS, TREATMENT AND EXPLANATIONS

If symptoms start to fade with neuroleptic medication, then this is
the time for further explanations and information for the sufferer
and family. These should include:

(1) A brief explanation about what we know of this cluster of
symptoms that we refer to as an acute schizophrenic episode;
the now reduced but nevertheless real risk of the sufferer
developing a more serious form of the illness; the importance
of the medication and the reasons for careful monitoring and
possible adjustment of the dosage; a discussion on side-
effects weighed against risks of discontinuing the drugs; a
discussion on diet and the benefits of cutting out refined

carbohydrates (and also wheat and other gluten-containing cereals if there has been a pronounced tendency to 'wolf down' stodgy foods).[4]

(2) A discussion of the sorts of symptom found in a schizophrenic illness, drawing on the individual concerned to give examples of his or her experiences as much as possible; the sorts of sign that may indicate the presence of such symptoms; factors that help, such as acceptance, patience and reassurance; factors that can exacerbate symptoms, such as the taking of street drugs, too high expectations from others and a premature change of or return to work or college.

(3) A discussion on the sorts of symptom/sign that might herald a threatened relapse. Any remaining queries or doubts. It may well be necessary at this stage to reinforce and go through again some of the points raised earlier. Some straightforward reading on the subject will usually be welcomed and in the first instance there is an inexpensive leaflet which can be particularly useful, entitled *Psychiatric Diagnosis*;[5] this is obtainable from the National Schizophrenia Fellowship, together with a recommended reading list.

Such an approach will involve one or two professionals in several meetings with the sufferer and the family, but this is time that pays dividends in terms of prevention and the maintaining of good health. Moreover, this approach has the advantage of alerting all concerned to the risks involved at a time when they can still be protected from much, or all, of the stigma of a diagnosis of schizophrenia.

BREAKDOWN – MINIMIZING THE SUFFERING

Where the illness has gone past the early stages discussed above, or where there has been a first or second breakdown, then the sufferer will usually be admitted to hospital or supervised in a day hospital or similar resource. At present, it is rare to find any work carried out in these settings which is aimed *specifically at relieving a schizophrenic illness or preventing future attacks*, other than, of course, the adjusting and monitoring of medication. There is so much else that could be done and that should be almost mandatory at this stage in a schizophrenic illness. Sufferers need help in separating reality from a nightmare world of fantasy. They need relief from the torment of feelings of distorted guilt and worthlessness. They need information about what is happening to them. They need stimulating activities and the reintroduction of structure to their daily lives right from the start. If all of this is provided, then they should come out of their illness with a chance of survival and staying well. Let us take a look at ways of achieving these primary objectives.

COMMUNICATION

Most schizophrenic patients come into hospital beset with delusionary, and maybe paranoid, ideas. One sufferer asked me recently:

Why couldn't they have explained where I was when they admitted me? I was told it was a hospital, but knew that it couldn't be so because everyone was fully dressed, most of them watching television, and there were no beds nor nurses in sight. This all fed into my delusionary system and it took weeks for me to accept that nurses out of uniform were in fact nurses and that this was a kind of hospital.[6]

Not unnaturally, this extra confusion slowed up this young man's recovery because he immediately regarded those who welcomed him into the ward as lying to him, and, therefore, as enemies. He now suggests that if he had been given a simple explanation of the type of hospital this was and told that it catered for people with the sorts of mental health problem which usually respond well to medication, he would have been better able to sort out reality from fantasy and more ready eventually to accept help. Although this all seems obvious when put this way, I am not sure that any of us would automatically recognize the need for spelling out this sort of straightforward explanation. However, we really should do so; we must *keep talking* with sufferers when they are psychotic and repeating simple matter-of-fact statements that will help them make sense of what is happening to them. Too often, they complain that no one refers to their diagnosis nor talks with them about how they are feeling when they are in hospital. The implications of such silence are enormous. One very well woman, who has given talks to professionals around the country, points out that the patient then feels *less than human* and decides, 'I must be a hopeless case because no one will discuss my problems or give me any chance to respond intelligently.'[7] As it is common for sufferers to be overwhelmed with feelings of distorted guilt and worthlessness, this avoidance of any attempt at meaningful discussion with them is really quite destructive. It is important that those working with them should be aware of this.

REALITY-TESTING

There seems to be little understanding of the need for constant reassurance for individuals experiencing hallucinations and delusionary thoughts as they struggle to regain their grasp on reality. They need constant opportunities to 'test reality' out with the help of members of staff. This can be time-consuming, but also very rewarding as the benefit obtained by the patient is so obvious. Sufferers need to be able to question a trusted listener every time they believe they may be hallucinating and every time they are beset with delusional ideas. If they can discuss their doubts each time they occur, and if they know that the listener will never be tempted to dodge the issue, or casually brush away their fears, then they can gain real strength from reassurance. In this way, psychotic sufferers can become less confused and frightened and also very much encouraged by a regular human contact all too often lacking in their stay in hospital. More often than not, such exchanges take no more than a few minutes, but during the worst stages of a breakdown their calming influence will be very temporary and will be followed by frequent requests for further reassurance. These should be recognized as a sign of need rather than manifestations of 'attention-seeking' or 'manipulating' behaviour!

Such an approach can be used outside as well as inside a hospital setting and indeed I have described elsewhere[8] how I first introduced this method of working by using it with a young sufferer in the community. We drew up a contract between her and her parents that every time she thought she heard their 'voices' cursing and abusing her (her most troublesome symptom) she would challenge them. Her parents in turn promised always to find time to respond seriously to these desperate calls for help. They found this much more painful than they imagined and it brought home to them for just how long these cruel symptoms can persist in a seemingly well young woman. She now regards this work, which lasted for several years and enabled her to distinguish between reality and residual symptoms, as a vital part of her full recovery; it was she who called this approach 'reality-testing'.

EDUCATIONAL PROGRAMME

Once patients are beginning to regain their grasp of reality, with the help of the right medication and by 'reality-testing' with the staff, then they should be provided with information about their illness and ways to cope with it. Falloon and Talbot report one interesting example of this approach in the United States,[9] including the provision of regular seminars for recovering patients on matters such as their diagnosis, and the possible cause and course of the illness. Emphasis was given to the rationale for using medication, consideration of side-effects and how to deal with them, developing cues for prompting tablet-taking, which involved relatives where possible. This seems to be a sensible approach to the giving and sharing of information.

A SPECIAL KIND OF GROUPWORK

At this point groupwork aimed exclusively at individuals with this illness (for recovering sufferers still on the ward, together, perhaps, with others who have been discharged and are further on the road to recovery) can be invaluable. The emphasis of such work should be on encouraging discussion of symptoms which enables 'reality-testing' to take place together with the sharing of ways of coping. Such a group can help repair a damaged self-image by providing a sense of belonging. It can help to revive communication skills, and also provides the right kind of stimulation. An added bonus can be the forming of relationships that may survive long after recovery;

relationships in which it is safe to discuss the special problems for sufferers of coping with everyday life.

STIMULATION AND REST

Other 'musts' during a sufferer's stay in hospital include a programme of activities that he or she finds stimulating, preferably for short spells each day. These should be interspersed with *adequate rest* as most sufferers experience very real mental and physical exhaustion during, and for some time after, a schizophrenic illness. There is a fine line between over- and under-activity which can be very difficult to determine, but it is my experience that sufferers are not helped by hours of inactivity and boredom. Some list this as their main objection to a previous stay in hospital, and this seems to be the case more often now that the hospitals are being run down. On the other hand, it is rather sad to find wards where patients are refused admission to their dormitories or bedrooms during the daytime. 'Rest' is not a dirty word; it is a healing process so long as it is part of a structured programme. Patients who have a serious illness may well appreciate a sleep after their midday meal, for example. Many of the rest of us do, without needing the excuse of being unwell! I know sufferers whose symptoms are clearly exacerbated by a lack of opportunity to have any peace and quiet during the day, let alone a short sleep. Stimulation followed by opportunities to rest are important features of a structured daily routine that can then be continued after discharge from hospital.

DISCHARGE AND AFTER-CARE

All those sufferers who have even just one schizophrenic breakdown should be regarded as potentially needing *continuing care* of some sort, and their families as deserving of and needing ongoing support. All should be involved in the initial family sessions discussed earlier in this chapter and all should have recourse to a named professional on the end of a telephone *at the very least*. This applies, of course, to their close relatives as well.

Involved professionals should stress the length of time it can take to make a proper recovery, and for the need for all concerned to be content initially with small successes which will lead to a gradually repaired self-esteem. This should be reinforced from time to time, so that sufferers do not lose patience together with faith in their treatment and families are not deceived by an apparent, premature, recovery. Sufferers should be given opportunities to talk, preferably in a group situation, about matters that raise problems for them, such as coping with residual symptoms as well as with society's attitudes to mental illness. If they are not well enough to work, then they should be persuaded to get involved in some sort of organized activity for part of each day *from the start*. Day centres, adult education classes or various types of voluntary work are examples of such activities. The important thing is that there should be regular involvement if a gradual deterioration is to be avoided. Wing aptly describes the fine balance that needs to be achieved:

On the one hand, too much social stimulation, experienced by the patient as *social intrusiveness*, may lead to an acute relapse. On the other hand, too little stimulation will exacerbate any tendency already present towards social withdrawal, slowness, underactivity, and an apparent lack of motivation.[10]

Finally, and most importantly, both ongoing medical supervision and a 'lifeline' in case of any sign of deterioration are a must. Good practice at this stage can help to prevent yet another sufferer returning to hospital again and again.

'REVOLVING DOOR' SYNDROME

For those who are already caught up in these frequent readmissions, we should be finding out from the sufferers and their carers what goes wrong for them and what tends to happen before each further breakdown. For example, we know that those closest to sufferers do notice early signs of relapse before others do, so are they and sufferers being listened to while the latter *will still agree to any necessary adjustment to medication*? Where sufferers still have the support of families, are the latter getting enough professional back-up? Do they need help with stress management or with developing problem-solving skills within the home? Jackie Ferris and Faye Wilson quote one mother's predicament:

Well, he's home now and they told me on the ward that he's schizophrenic. I'm not sure what that means but I do know that for my son it's like being in a cage that's made of glass, but the thing is society seems to have locked us in there, too. We can see the people outside, I'm shouting for help and they pass by, social workers, doctors, nurses. I can't make them hear what it's like for me or get them to unlock the door with their knowledge and understanding. . . . There must be a right way to do it but nobody's told me yet. I'm just the one who has him day in day out. I want to help him but I need to know how . . . can you let me know where to go from here and call in to see me sometime? My family won't come any more.[11]

This sort of cry from the wilderness is not unusual and it does suggest that we have not come very far along the road from the days when families were shunned as the cause of the sufferer's distress. Dafydd Huws, psychiatrist, protests that 'We should certainly lay this cruel myth that many thousands of families have been allowed to think they contributed towards their children's illness; we have evidence now that this is wholly untrue,'[12] and Jennifer Newton, commenting on her research sponsored by MIND, says that 'Relatives complain that they get the blame for the illness. . . . This lack of sensitivity, in addition to not giving relatives enough information, can contribute towards a patient's relapse.'[13]

We must all start to work together if such carers are to persevere with supporting the sufferer. They should be treated as part of the primary care team; they are in any event providing most of the care. Let us ask them what they think goes wrong each time their relatives relapse, and what they feel could help to prevent this happening again and again, and then work with them to protect these vulnerable sufferers.

Are those without families to support them being monitored carefully enough by professionals keeping a check on their medication and watching out for early signs of deterioration? Are they getting enough support in the community and are their living conditions creating too many day-to-day problems? What sort of 'quality of life' are they enjoying? How much do they understand about their illness, and about their vulnerability to relapse? Let us ask them what sort of help they would like to be receiving (as against what may be available), and let us find out what they think goes wrong each time they relapse.

When these 'revolving door' patients start to relapse, they should be treated before it is necessary to think of having to use the mental health legislation. Where this is not viable, then they should be admitted on section *in the interests of their health* sooner rather than later. The trauma of long delays, often avoidable, are increasingly causing anguish and despair for families and others in the community as well as contributing to the visible deterioration of the sufferers themselves. Perhaps we need to examine the connotations we associate with the words *treatment and discharge* when we are considering this type of patient. With all serious mental illness, we have to add the words *and continuing care*. The York Survey[14] found that community psychiatric nurses and social workers would visit for a while after the patient's discharge, but, burdened by fresh cases all the time, this contact usually lasted only three to six months. Clearly, this sort of temporary help is not appropriate with individuals who are prone to recurring schizophrenic breakdowns. Let us acknowledge this and press for more human resources where there are too few, or for the redirecting of existing ones from preoccupation with the 'worried well' where appropriate.

VIOLENCE

Before we leave the discussion on care in the community of those individuals who suffer with the positive symptoms of schizophrenia, we should consider one problem which can make it like a nightmare for those concerned. Although this illness hits the headlines when some violent crime has been committed, such behaviour is not a typical characteristic of schizophrenia and is more usually associated with having a certain type of personality rather than with suffering from this illness. However, there is no doubt that *uncontrolled* psychosis can lead to violent behaviour. Unrelieved hallucinations and delusions can bring overwhelming frustration and terror with them. If, and when, sufferers strike out at others, it is usually because they believe that they are under threat or attack. Because others are unaware of the delusional ideas – are not in fact sharing the individual's psychotic nightmare – then any violence appears to be unprovoked. The fact that this is rarely the case, however, does not make the danger any less real, and all those working with this illness have a real responsibility to watch out for warning signs of breakdown or relapse. In particular, the professionals concerned should be listening to any fears expressed by carers and/or relatives and also be sensitive to any signs of nervousness or tenseness in them. This is very important as sometimes there is collusion with a potentially aggressive sufferer, in some cases through loyalty and in others through fear.

Clearly, every attempt must be made to find a way to control the sufferer's symptoms and to maintain this. However, there are a few cases where seemingly this cannot be achieved, either because the available drugs do not suit the individual or because his or her cooperation cannot be won and maintained. In such cases and where there is unpredictable violent behaviour which puts others at risk, then it is not usually appropriate for the sufferer to live in unsupervised accommodation. Occasionally it may be that the provision of such a resource will not suffice and that the individual's freedom will then have to be curtailed, albeit temporarily. It may also be necessary to make firm rules, including measures such as the taking out of injunctions by close relatives to put their homes 'out of bounds' to the sufferer. Fortunately such instances are not common, but it is not acceptable for everyone to turn the other way as sometimes happens when a lone mother, say, lives in terror of the dreaded knock at the door. If her fears are justified, then she has the right to be protected and may need to be encouraged to take out an injunction, or take whatever other action is required, and *she must be supported in this.* Perhaps we can imagine just how painful taking such steps might be for a mother who knows that it is an illness that has made her son or daughter into a violent stranger?

Rather differently, it is not unknown to come across a household 'tyrannized' by the unreasonable demands of an unwell sufferer. This can happen when, for example, relatives feel they should 'pander' to every whim of the individual because he or she is ill (guaranteed to bring the worst out in all of us!) or if they fear there may be aggressive behaviour if they say 'No'. Once revealed, this sort of situation can usually be resolved, as this is behaviour which has been learned and unwittingly encouraged rather than behaviour which is provoked by overwhelming frustration or terror. It is not acceptable and it should not be tolerated. However, intensive support and monitoring will be necessary initially, to enable the setting up of 'house rules' so that all those concerned may live as normal a life as possible.

THE TYPE II SYNDROME

What can be done to help those who have developed the type of schizophrenic illness that will to a greater or lesser extent have dulled their emotional responses and damaged their social skills and their intellectual potential? It has been recorded again and again that those families who continue to support their relatives find this type of altered behaviour the most difficult to tolerate. This sort of drastic change of personality can provoke feelings of loss and frustration, with families complaining that the sufferer just sleeps all day, or sits and stares at the wall, and shows no interest in what is going on around him or her. For the lone supporting relative, perhaps the mother or the spouse, the sufferer's handicap can be so profound that it amounts to a bereavement, with the withdrawal of companionship and emotional support in a previously familiar personality. The loss is very real and may be compared with that of losing a loved one by death. However, the usual mourning process by which we eventually may adjust healthily to such loss is not available to these carers. The person being mourned is not dead; the pain of the loss does not gradually ease with time, nor do the anger and the feelings of guilt which are all part of a normal mourning. No wonder it is more comfortable for others to turn away in the face of such suffering. This will not do. If we do not want these people to give up on caring, then we must offer them something; we must try harder to identify with their sorrow and pain and find some way of helping them and their relatives.

It is my experience that the chronically ill sufferer can be persuaded to come along with a trusted professional to some sort of appropriate resource, giving the carer(s) a break and providing a little stimulation for the individual as well. This will only happen if someone takes the trouble to call, and 'fetch and carry' regularly for a while, but the effort is well justified and the opportunity can then be made to spend some time with the carer(s) before or after the outing, albeit *just listening*. Better still, I have found that providing a resource, such as a social club, for both carers and sufferers can be seen as more attractive to these families. This way, relatives can have a regular outing that allows the sufferer to mix with his or her peers while they also have a rare chance to socialize and meet with other carers.

Surprisingly, even including such sufferers in groupwork aimed at less handicapped individuals is well worth considering. I have seen one or two 'open up' in such a group on rare occasions. Their contributions have been exactly what was needed at the time to help another member and have demonstrated just how aware they really are about what is going on around them. I have also seen several lasting relationships develop, and these make up in loyalty and respect for what they might lack in excitement and emotion. Social contacts of this sort serve to provide much-needed stimulation for sufferers and can also make life a little more rewarding for carers.

THE CLIENT SPEAKS!

Two well-recovered sufferers may have an important contribution to make to this discussion on the ways that professionals can help people with this illness. One points out that 'It is essential that *hope* is held on to alongside awareness that getting better is a process that takes time. Meanwhile, smaller, attainable goals are necessary to produce small successes, increasing self-esteem and further hope.'[5] The other stood up on a platform recently and made a powerful plea to all those who work with schizophrenia, saying, 'However scarce the resources available to you, please, above all, introduce sufferers to other sufferers';[16] a powerful argument, perhaps, for bringing this illness out into the open? Similarly, of course, some relatives very much appreciate being introduced to local self-help groups such as those provided by the National Schizophrenia Fellowship.

SUMMING UP

Most of this book has described an approach to schizophrenia that had led to avoidable despair and waste of potential. Perhaps the word 'approach' is a misnomer; we have in fact *distanced* ourselves from the truth and from what really happens in this illness and, in so doing, from its victims. What, then, is the main thrust of the recommendations evolving from the discussion in this and the last chapter? It might be helpful to itemize them:

(1) Education for all.

(2) Early assessment and recognition.

(3) Early diagnosis (albeit sometimes tentative) and acknowledgment.

(4) More readiness to use the drugs that relieve some of the symptoms common to all psychotic illnesses, but particularly schizophrenia, together with a real appreciation of differing individual needs in so far as dosage is concerned.

(5) Explanations and information for sufferers and those who matter to them.

(6) Intensive work with sufferers from the start, enabling *reality-testing* and insight into illness, together with understanding of future vulnerability.

(7) Adequate stimulation and rest throughout illness and recovery.

(8) Proper follow-up and after-care.

(9) Introduction to self-help organizations, to relevant reading material and access to updates on research and available resources.

These, then, are some of the things we can do to minimize the devastation of schizophrenia. Its main strength is *our fear of it*. Instead of formulating a sensible defence strategy, we turn away, hoping it will do so as well. Meanwhile, the illness continues to strike down victims who are deprived of the benefit of immediate attention and care. This really makes no sense at all; imagine a commanding officer who gives an order that results in some of his men getting wounded, and who then decides not to go back to rescue them because it is just too awful to contemplate their suffering! Until we have the courage to face up to this illness and begin to understand the need for prompt treatment, we shall go on failing some of our finest young people miserably (to our own cost as well as theirs). Naomi Smith, a nurse for many years, has commented:

At best, future generations may be perplexed by our ignorance and lack of humanity. They will wonder why the medical professionals, and particularly the psychiatrists, did not have more fire in their bellies, did not make more effort to lessen the heart-break of patients and their families and did not spread the knowledge they had more widely.[17]

Future generations will indeed be perplexed, as are some of the present one. In this chapter, we have looked at factors which could dramatically reduce the present level of misery and suffering. This is only the beginning; we all have a part to play in making this happen. The next, and final, chapter takes a look at how it can be achieved.

10 · Getting It Right

In December 1986, the Chair of the Social Services Select Committee of the House of Commons commented:

Schizophrenia is a major mental illness that has been under-resourced. The needs are not recognized and the services are poor. Professional support takes a lot of time, and general practitioners and social workers have neither the time nor the resources to offer ongoing care either to the patients or to their families. . . . What is needed is continuing care, which provides different choices, depending on the state of the illness.[1]

There can be little doubt that the much-heralded 'community care' has come to have a very hollow ring about it, and increasingly there is talk about the need for 'continuing care' which is a concept most of us can better define. It is becoming clear that community care for the seriously mentally ill is little more than an ideological concept based on at least two fantasies: first, that releasing long-term patients from hospital will absolve their difficulties, and second, that a loving society will eagerly welcome and cherish them. The reality, as we have seen, is very different. However, with the right sort of help and support, and with *continuing care*, many schizophrenia sufferers could find a reasonable quality of life in the community. Let us take a look now at some of the areas where we might all contribute to making this happen.

RESEARCH

It would seem to be remarkable that one of the most serious illnesses known to mankind and one which strikes down young people in the prime of life attracts just 0.5 per cent of the UK's Medical Research Council's funds.[2] Moreover, at the time of writing there are plans to close down the Clinical Research Centre at Northwick Park Hospital which has played a constant and vital role in so much of research into this illness over the past decade. During the 1980s, the Dean of the Institute of Psychiatry pointed out:

Prospects for advances in our understanding of schizophrenia have never been brighter. Recent research has shown that the disorder can be caused either by a single abnormal gene or by subtle brain damage at, or before, birth. It will be a tragedy if lack of support for research prevents us translating this new knowledge into improved treatment for sufferers.[3]

So many urgent questions are begging for answers right now. We need to know more about these two probable main causes of the illness. We need to identify the various sub-groups of sufferers, to understand the role of street drugs, and cannabis in particular, to assess the importance of diet for some individuals, and to find explanations for the high incidence of diagnosed schizophrenia amongst 'second generation' West Indian males in the UK. These are just a few of the urgent considerations waiting to be addressed . . .

Perhaps we should not be too surprised at the Medical Research Council's modest contribution to this major problem if we consider that schizophrenia attracts only 1 per cent of all the monies donated to charity.[4] It may very well be that depressing statistics like these merely demonstrate the success of a remarkable conspiracy of silence about a forgotten illness. If so, perhaps we could all start to redress the balance by giving some of our money, or time and support, to bodies such as SANE, the National Schizophrenia Fellowship and the Schizophrenia Association of Great Britain (see Useful Addresses at end of book)? Perhaps we should also agitate for more of the publicly funded Medical Research Council's wealth to reach this neglected cause? Let's do it!

MENTAL HEALTH LEGISLATION

We have noted that the Mental Health Act 1983 has been referred to as 'an eviction order for schizophrenics',[5] although they make up the majority of individuals who are meant to be catered for by this legislation. The emphasis is on 'negative' rights, described by Kathleen Jones as 'the rights *not* to be categorized as mentally ill, *not* to be committed to hospital, *not* to receive treatment'.[6] Perhaps just one example will illustrate this emphasis. When patients arrive in hospital, usually following sincere attempts by the professionals concerned to persuade them that they are ill and needing treatment; the present legislation requires them to be invited *to appeal against having been sectioned.* This would confuse someone in good health; it hardly helps psychotic patients regain a grip on reality! Neither does it negate paranoid ideas of having been 'got at and put away' for others' convenience. These appeals lead to tribunal hearings usually around half-way through the duration of the section; this means that patients who appeal and who are on a twenty-eight-day section, for example, and all those concerned with them, have to negotiate the bureaucratic process of a legal hearing during the first fortnight of treatment. Hard-pressed members of the psychiatric profession and hospital social workers spend a great deal of their time preparing the necessary paperwork and attending tribunal hearings rather than with patients. These hearings sometimes last several hours; lawyers are increasingly involved in matters pertaining to mental illness. Quite apart from what can be hassle and stress for the patient and anxious relatives, there is a real risk that the patient will be discharged by the tribunal before the supervising doctor feels this is justified. It usually takes longer than two weeks or so to stabilize patients adequately for survival in the community. Similarly, it is not uncommon for patients on Section 3 (a six-month section), which is used for those whose effective treatment will take longer, to be discharged by a tribunal after, say, three months and before the supervising doctor would recommend this. Such reluctance of hospital doctors to discharge a patient too soon should be considered in the context of the pressing problems incurred for them by an acute shortage of available beds. Perhaps the most amazing feature of the tribunal system is that the three members of each panel – a lawyer, a doctor and a layperson – receive no feedback on the results of the decisions they make. They do not hear of the avoidable tragedies that take place and therefore cannot learn from their experiences during their three-year 'stint' with the mental health tribunal system; surely not an ideal illustration of 'ignorance is bliss'?

We have noted that one of the biggest problems with the Mental Health Act 1983, in so far as it affects schizophrenia, is the interpretation of the grounds for admission to hospital by so many of the professionals who use it. The widespread ignorance of the fact that it allows for admission to hospital 'in the interests of [the patient's] health'[7] is a scandal. At the time of writing, there are calls for amendments to the new Code of Practice,[8] laid before Parliament and accepted at the end of 1989, to address this issue specifically and also to lay more stress on the responsibility of hospital managers securely to detain sectioned patients who may be a risk to themselves or others.

Another matter which has failed to be resolved since the advent of the Mental Health Act 1983 is the need for the provision of some sort of compulsory treatment order in the community. A small but important group of 'revolving door' patients respond dramatically to neuroleptic drug treatment but never seem to gain insight into this. When they are discharged from hospital they feel well and they stop taking their medication; very quickly they start to deteriorate again, to the despair of themselves and all those involved with them. Eventually they become so ill that they are admitted to hospital again. These potentially well sufferers experience one failure after another and their unhappy lives are punctuated by traumatic admissions to hospital for what amounts to temporary first aid. Under the previous mental health legislation patients could be discharged on a six-month section and this could be renewed as necessary. This approach had the dual advantage of keeping professionals involved with the monitoring of the health of these particularly vulnerable sufferers and of being able to bring them back into hospital for treatment, under the prevailing section, if they showed signs of relapse through continuing to refuse medication. This is not permitted under the new legislation and a London-based psychiatrist who specializes in treating patients in the community has commented:

So we are in the position of having to watch patients relapse, usually because they are refusing medication, until they are ill enough to be admitted under a section . . . relatives have to wait helplessly, watching the patient's condition deteriorate, while having to endure the consequent disruption of their lives, social embarrassment and sometimes violent behaviour . . .[9]

And so, at a time when hospital beds are increasingly at a premium and more and more sufferers are expected to survive in the community, we have lost one more preventive tool. Although this matter has been the cause of grave concern for several years, and the subject of continuous academic debate, up until now the many factions involved with this illness have been unable to agree on any course of action to be recommended to the government of the day. It must surely be high time for differences to be put aside so that everyone can focus on the matter in question; how do we keep this important minority of sufferers well and how do we protect carers and others who may be involved from such indefensible anguish? Meanwhile, the despair continues.

While on this difficult subject of compulsory treatment, it is revealing and worthy of note that there are some sufferers who are concerned with a very different sort of 'right' to the ones with which the mental health legislation is so concerned. Having kept well for years on appropriate treatment, they are anxious to find a way of ensuring that they will be prescribed appropriate and additional neuroleptic medication *immediately* in the event of their showing signs of relapse and becoming divorced from reality. Their insight into this illness makes them only too aware of their vulnerability should there be any delay over getting this sort of help. They know the sort of problems that can arise *once they are psychotic* and they have no wish to go through the nightmare of another breakdown nor to risk the damage it could cause. Perhaps some of the lawyers now so involved with mental health matters could investigate ways of achieving some kind of protection of this kind? We are, of course, now talking about a 'positive' right; *the right to make sure one is not denied treatment when it is needed.* What are the others?

'POSITIVE' RIGHTS

Members of the VOICES forum and of the National Schizophrenia Fellowship have recently produced a Charter of Rights[10] that pinpoints the main issues that should concern us if we really want to focus on protecting sufferers' *positive* rights rather than the rights of denial and neglect. Really these fall into three categories:

(a) Those that rely on the rest of society changing its attitudes to mental illness and to the mentally ill, that is, an end to stigma and discrimination.

(b) Those that add up to a rewarding lifestyle, with adequate material comforts, that is, appropriate employment or occupation, adequate income and acceptable accommodation.

(c) Those that recognize society's responsibility to provide caring and protection, that is, available treatment and asylum when they are needed.

Let us look at each of these areas in turn.

STIGMA

We have talked about the need for *acceptance* and acknowledgment of this illness, but sufferers need to know that they too are accepted. Being accepted implies being valued and being entitled to all the choices that the rest of society enjoys. Until we all do something about the stigma attached to this illness, these choices will not be available to a quarter of a million people in the UK alone. We will know we are winning when sufferers and families are able to talk openly about schizophrenia. We sometimes seem to be a long way off that at the present time. Anyone who has tried to open new resources in the community for the mentally ill will know that there is usually active opposition to this from various sections of the local population. Although this is based on fear and ignorance, there is nevertheless an amazing amount of vocal hostility expressed by such people. Until we set about sharing information and educating the younger members of our society, then things are not likely to change. Meanwhile, this hostility not only slows down the provision of viable alternatives to scarce hospital beds; it also serves to escalate feelings of isolation and pain in sufferers and their families. It is significant that most such opposition dies down very quickly when the home, hostel or day centre has been open for a short while, proving that having a psychiatric history does not make one a bad neighbour.

DISCRIMINATION

Chris Heginbotham, a former director of MIND, has pointed out that mentally ill people particularly suffer extreme forms of discrimination, adding: 'Few people realize that there is no redress for disabled people. No equivalent of the Sex Discrimination Act or the Race Relations Act exists and any disabled person can be discriminated against with impunity.'[11]

Consider the example of the young man who has painstakingly made a full recovery from a schizophrenic breakdown five years ago. Since then, he has held down a couple of part-time jobs and obtained a good honours degree. He now seeks work which is appropriate to his ability and his qualifications, that is, probably pensionable employment. If he answers the questions on the job application form truthfully, he will be fortunate indeed if he gets past the doctor employed to protect the organization's pension scheme. This doctor will often be one who knows little if anything about mental illness, and even less about the magnitude of this candidate's achievements to date. Quite simply, the latter will be considered a pension risk and will almost certainly be rejected without interview. As psychiatrists have attempted to protect their patients from this sort of discrimination, so employers have become more and more astute, so that if candidates innocently claim that they have had a mild depression, or an adolescent disturbance, or whatever, then their answer to the next question, 'Do you take any medication?' will often tell them what they want to know. Small wonder that it has become common practice for many of those who work with sufferers to suggest, albeit reluctantly, that they should be reticent about their medical history. Naomi Smith comments: 'Now, if I am asked, I advise my schizophrenic friends not always to admit that they have or have had this diagnosis. Our society does not always deserve to be told the truth.'[12]

There is no doubt at all that some very able people – remember, these are the very individuals who have often shown enormous tenacity and strength of character to win through – will not get suitable employment without holding back information about their past. This in turn can put an intolerable stress on them. Few of us function well under such conditions; the slightest sign of time off for anything other than a physical problem can lead to instant dismissal. Many sufferers have been sacked for denying their mental health record on their application forms, despite a good work record up to the point of this coming to light. This is a real 'Catch 22' situation; well-recovered sufferers need fulfilling employment to have any sort of quality of life and yet society frequently denies them the opportunity to achieve this. While employers cannot protect themselves from all those individuals who will have a first breakdown tomorrow, or those seemingly fit employees who take regular sick leave (an increasingly common phenonemon), most of them reject out-of-hand people who have had a schizophrenic breakdown even though they have clearly demonstrated their ability and determination to stay well. Just to put the problem of people with this illness into context, it is interesting to note that those citizens who break the law are protected from having to declare their criminal record after five years have expired, but there is no such reprieve for those who have had a mental illness. *Isn't it about time that we started getting our priorities right?* If employers do not need to know about 'spent' criminal records, then they do not need to know about psychiatric records either. Existing built-in safeguards, such as the requirement to provide suitable references and the use of introductory probationary periods, should suffice. There are a few employers, such as some Civil Service departments, who do offer jobs to suitable candidates regardless of their health history. Presumably they find such an enlightened policy worthwhile; certainly many of my clients proved themselves very employable during the time that the Community Programme was in operation, and several of them were promoted to supervisory positions. The two features that provided the opportunity for such achievement were (a) applicants' health records did not count against them, and (b) employees could start on a part-time basis and graduate to more hours as and when appropriate.

Discrimination against individuals who have a psychiatric history does not stop with restricted employment opportunities. People with a mental health record have difficulties obtaining visas, are unlikely to have an opportunity to emigrate and have difficulty in obtaining insurance cover of all kinds (paying well over the odds for their usually non-life threatening diagnosis). Furthermore, if they have a chronic schizophrenic illness or are part of the 'revolving door' syndrome, they may even find themselves taken off their GP's list and have difficulty in finding a new doctor who will take them on.

OCCUPATION

As we have noted, some sufferers are well enough to be gainfully employed on the open market and there is no reason why they should not achieve this if employers do not discriminate against them. Some are particularly suited to night work because of a lingering 'upturned twenty-four-hour clock' and are unlikely to seek work that starts early in the morning! Many sufferers would like to work but are unlikely ever to be able to cope with a full-time job. For them, and for those just recovered from an acute breakdown, it would be helpful if there were more part-time jobs available. This, of course, would suit other sections of the population such as young mothers, and 'job-share' opportunities are gradually becoming more common. There is a minority of sufferers who are not well enough to compete on the open market, but who nevertheless like to work and who thrive in sheltered employment. We need more sheltered workshops, such as those which were traditionally attached to the large hospitals, but even these are tending to disappear now that the hospitals are closing. This is a pity as such individuals find self-respect and contentment in doing a day's work within their own capabilities; something, I suspect, with which most of the rest of us can identify.

Finally, for those recovering from an acute breakdown as well as for many chronic sufferers who could not cope with a work situation, there is a pressing need for some sort of stimulating activity every day. At present, far too many of both categories of sufferers are languishing at home doing nothing and becoming less well because of it. We have discussed the sort of resources that are needed, and everyone involved with such individuals needs to pester their local Social Services departments and Health Authorities relentlessly until such facilities are made available for them . . .

ACCOMMODATION

I know no healthy individual who would wish to contemplate living in 'bed and breakfast' accommodation for a brief period, let alone indefinitely. It is a scandal that public taxes go to paying for this sort of lifestyle for members of our society who have more need for and, arguably, more right to superior housing than the rest of us! We can be fairly certain that this state of affairs will continue until the public demands a change and central government gives some sort of incentive to local government to build more suitable accommo-dation for people with a serious mental illness. I have constantly campaigned for the sort of living situation that one sufferer recommended several years ago:

A bed-sitting-room with adjoining kitchen and bathroom, with a commu-nal sitting-room . . . where one good meal a day is served, to be situated in a house with about eight other people residing . . . the people to be carefully selected so that all are compatible, the house to be in a quiet locale near the town centre, with a visiting nurse or doctor once a week.[13]

Many sufferers I have met would survive very much better than they do now and enjoy an improved quality of life in such a setting. Others would manage equally well with rather less support, in reasonable bed-sitters/single flatlets with a communal room and a warden to keep an eye on them. This sort of accommodation is regularly provided for the elderly but hardly ever for vulnerable young schizophrenia sufferers. Better still, the implementation of what we call 'core and cluster' accommodation would combine the advantages of this type of accommodation with readily available opportunities for socializing and supervision. With this, units such as the bed-sitters or flatlets described above are provided in the near vicinity of a hostel or day centre and the tenants can use this 'core' resource and have ready access to its staff. Perhaps because of lack of financing, this attractive and practical provision is rare at the present time. The all too frequent alternatives of isolated 'tower block' bedsitters and 'bed and breakfast' are surely indictments on our society. Sadly, some individuals with this serious illness have less than this, sleeping in cardboard boxes on our streets. *Are we really prepared to settle for these sorts of standards in our affluent society?*

INCOME

For those who are not able to support themselves in open employment, the benefits system is a veritable jungle and the type and amount of benefit that any one sufferer receives depends on a bewildering number of factors. Some find themselves on disablement pensions of one kind or another and others find themselves on means-tested benefits. Others fall by the wayside because they cannot understand the system. Despite claims by the government of the day that this has been simplified, it has in fact become so complicated that for those who are entitled to help with rented or 'bed and breakfast' accommodation, it is a triumph when anyone manages to sort it out before the accommodation or the individual has gone! Social workers blanch when they contemplate a typical DSS or local authority housing benefits form.

More importantly, there has been a gradual erosion of standards of living during the 1980s for those who have to rely on state benefits, and these include many schizophrenia sufferers who have little hope of ever escaping from this depressing poverty trap. Moreover, the complexity and inadequacy of our current welfare benefits scheme lead to many sick individuals dropping out of the system and ending up on the streets or, as we have seen, in prison. A recent report by the Social Security Advisory Committee has stated: 'Disabled people have a right to an adequate basic income which allows them to support themselves from the social security system and extra financial help to cover their special needs resulting from disability.'[4] Indeed, receipt of a single basic benefit recognizing the right to a decent standard of living, together with free prescriptions for necessary medicine, would be a reform that would greatly cut down the day-to-day hassle of being a schizophrenia sufferer or a close relative of one. Another privilege that would make all the difference to many sufferers' quality of life would be the provision of free or cheap travel on public transport, like that enjoyed by the physically and mentally handicapped. In a few enlightened areas where bus-passes are made available to the chronically mentally ill, I have seen these used with great initiative and enthusiasm. Where even a short bus trip becomes a luxury, then there is little chance of motivating these individuals to do more than sleep most of the day. Why should they not enjoy subsidized transport facilities that are available to other categories of the disabled?

TREATMENT

The right to treatment must be the most vital one for all those suffering with schizophrenia. The time when this matters most is when they are first developing a schizophrenic illness or if, and when, there is a threat of relapse. In both cases, early intervention is paramount. As we have seen, this is rarely available. It sometimes seems that so much energy and effort are going into preserving civil liberties (which can become irrelevant in the face of a psychotic illness) that there is none left for attempting effective preventive work.

There is an urgent need for GPs to have further opportunities for training in order to recognize the early signs of a developing illness. If these are not taken up, then perhaps we have to consider alternative measures such as (a) the provision of more readily available referral points which the public can be made aware of, such as mental health resource centres, or (b) the setting up of short training courses for those doctors who are prepared to give some of their practice time to specializing in mental health problems, offering readily available second opinions to patients and relatives feeling in need of these. There should be much more choice of specialized services available for patients and their families at times of threatened relapse. All too often, there is no choice at all, and many find themselves dependent on a psychiatrist and a team in whom they have learned to have no faith. This cannot be an acceptable state of affairs when the quality of supervision with an illness like schizophrenia can make the difference between survival and disaster. It seems at least possible that services would improve dramatically if patients and their carers could vote with their feet! Health authorities would quickly discover which specialist teams and which hospitals were providing an adequate service if we were not so hidebound by catchment areas and 'sectorization'. These do nothing at all to encourage the raising of standards and altering of attitudes at a time when such changes are surely essential.

NEED FOR ASYLUM

The final 'positive' right that has to be a top priority is the right to asylum at times of need. This is becoming more and more difficult to achieve, partly because of the shortage of hospital beds or alternative resources and partly because of over-concern with civil liberties issues by some psychiatrists, as well as others. Emma and Edward, whose stories were told in Chapter 7, were two very different examples of this phenomenon.

I know sufferers who are terrified that the closing of a local hospital might mean they will be denied asylum if and when they need it. Interestingly, a few of them have explained very vividly that to get this asylum they have to be detained compulsorily because their impulsive restlessness at such times makes it impossible for them to settle without this and they discharge themselves. Others are profoundly unhappy about the closure of their local hospital because they believe that nothing can replace its promise of sanctuary, the accessibility of so many resources and, above all, the peace and space to be found in the beautiful grounds. Other advantages that are mentioned are the sense of feeling part of a self-sufficient community and, for some, the sanctity of the hospital chapel where they feel welcome. By condemning all that was worst in the old institutions with their unpardonable abuses, we are in danger of ignoring, and losing, what was best in them. Some of today's remaining hospitals (and some of those now closed) are deeply valued by people with schizophrenia – the illness they cater for most. These hospitals are a far cry from the barrenness of isolated bedsitters, and 'bed and breakfast' land.

THE RIGHTS OF FAMILIES AND OTHERS IN THE COMMUNITY

Although it seems that we may have stopped blaming families for their relatives' schizophrenia, we have certainly not stopped abusing them. They, like carers of individuals with other disabilities, are a particularly neglected section of our society. Because there are people like this who will not reject their own, however great the sacrifice, society feels free to forget its obligations to them and currently does just that. These unpaid, untrained carers save the taxpayer enormous sums of money and receive no thanks for it. At a time when it is increasingly taken for granted that families should care, often unsupported, for sick relatives in the home, central government's financial policies seem to militate against them. Not only do families with schizophrenia have to battle with the injustices and incompetencies discussed throughout the book, they also have to pay handsomely for the privilege. Perhaps it is not surprising that the past few years have seen the emergence of several national carers' associations which are beginning to make the needs of their members heard at last. Meanwhile, the level of deprivation and suffering of so many of these families makes a mockery of the agitations of those who advocate civil rights for the mentally ill. What, for heavens sake, of the rights of those who stand by them 'in sickness and in health'? What of the rights of their neighbours and other fellow citizens? The more emphasis we put on the 'negative' rights of sufferers to avoid the treatment which they need if they are to stay well, then the more we abuse the rights of those who try to support them and the rights of the rest of the community. The King's Fund has recently published a pamphlet in conjunction with the Health Education Authority and the Department of Health, which sets out the basic needs of carers. It declares that 'services need to be planned for and with them'[15] and this has to be a step in the right direction. However, families of schizophrenia sufferers have one vital need which is specific to this illness and which is rarely being met at the present time; they need help for relapsing relatives *before they become psychotic* and start the downward spiral of deterioration and torment. A Member of Parliament has recently claimed:

There is no excuse for any group of patients ever to be disadvantaged because of faulty cooperation between agencies or professionals, yet this is precisely what can happen to people with schizophrenic breakdown in the community. We need clear guidelines and personal accountability by professionals and monitoring standards . . .[16]

Perhaps when we achieve such clear guidelines and personal accountability by professionals and monitoring standards, then reason may start to prevail. Meanwhile, it is rare to find any real continuity in the treatment and care of individuals who have a schizophrenic illness. As we have seen, services are geared into *reacting* to a crisis and administering first aid, rather than providing care aimed at avoiding such crisis situations. Communication between service providers often belies the meaning of the word, and when disaster strikes, no one, it seems, is responsible for the handling (or mishandling) of the case. After much hesitation and delay it does seem that the British government might now have taken aboard the main thrust of the recommendations of the Griffiths Report[17] on community care. In particular, this acknowledges the need for *continuing care*. The keeping of local registers, and the appointing of case managers and key workers for each vulnerable individual, are the admirable baseline for the new type of service scheduled to start, albeit gradually, from April 1991. All of this seems sensible and long overdue, but it is not at all clear if and how it can be implemented. Two ingredients seem to be missing at the time of writing: the identifying of the particular population to be serviced and the identifying of sources of finance with which to attempt it. Even as ministerial statements indicate that proper ongoing care is to be provided for everyone with a serious mental illness, there is increasing evidence of local authorities having to cut back on all sorts of existing general community services. A recent nationwide survey sponsored by SANE and the National Schizophrenia Fellowship found that 69 per cent of respondents did not feel that the government is providing sufficient community care for the mentally ill.[18] Perhaps the public is beginning to realize at last how far down the road we are to experiencing what is happening in the United States?

MAKING IT ALL WORK

This final chapter has been concerned with reforms that could make a lot of difference to the quality of life of most schizophrenia sufferers and their families. Some of these reforms will depend on funds being made available for new resources. Many of these could be paid for by monies being made from selling valuable hospital lands, and others could be usefully provided on these very sites. We shall continue to need sanctuaries or asylums of some sort; where better than in purpose-built units in some of the beautiful rural settings which most sufferers find so tranquil and therapeutic? Indeed, someone wrote recently:

There is a strong feeling that one day someone will come up with a new idea of providing a centre of caring and rehabilitation set in peaceful surroundings of beautiful grounds – in fact, a place just like the old long-stay mental hospital – a temporary asylum from the stresses of life.[19]

Some of the reforms advocated in this book will depend on government intervention and involve several ministries; measures such as a single basic payment for the disabled, better services for carers, the financing of the proposed system of caring for the long-term mentally ill, and, not least, a shift of emphasis back to a duty to provide treatment and caring in the mental health legislation. Most of these will only happen if and when governments discover that such matters concern electors. Many of the others will depend on the changing of attitudes. It is right that we should accept responsibility for the quality of life of vulnerable members of our community; the health of any society is deservedly judged on such values.

Perhaps the most important reforms of all will depend on those who work with sufferers being prepared to change direction and consider a preventive approach to schizophrenia. Chapter 9 spelled out the components of such an approach. The priorities are: *assessment, recognition, diagnosis, acknowledgment, prompt and appropriate drug treatment, explanations and information-giving, stimulation and reality-testing, followed by diligent after-care.* The aim is to prevent avoidable breakdown and damage. This is not happening at present. A quarter of a million individuals and some of their families are shouting for help; they want us to know of the terrible suffering that is their lot and they want us to know that much of this distress can be prevented.

The necessary leap into *preventive care* will only happen if there is a will for it to happen. It will only succeed if all those who work with this illness have the opportunity to acquire real knowledge about its symptoms and the responses these provoke. It will only happen when health professionals understand the potential for controlling a schizophrenic illness and the potential of sufferers to cope with their vulnerability and to survive. It will only happen when all those working with the mental health legislation understand the importance of early intervention and have the will to use the existing law to prevent suffering. It will only happen when we all brush away the cobwebs of the 1960s.[20] It will only happen when all of us care enough.

Hospital Visit

You brought me flowers
(I saw my grave)
You brought me smiles
(I saw you mock)
You gave advice
(Another plot)
You couldn't stay
(The other world)
You checked your watch
(Changed my time)

You stole my heart
Once, in another life
Not mine

You turned to look, as
You walked away
I stood helpless
Watching you

Heather S. Ashworth, VOICES

Do we care enough?

Notes and References

CHAPTER 2: WHAT HAPPENS IN SCHIZOPHRENIA?

1 North, Carol, MD, *Welcome, Silence* (London: Simon and Schuster, 1988).

2 For a detailed discussion, see Roderick Anscombe, 'The disorder of consciousness', *Schizophrenia Bulletin*, vol. 13, no. 2 (1987).

3 Hemsley, D. R., 'A two stage model of attention in schizophrenia research', *British Journal of Social and Clinical Psychology*, 14 (1975), 81–9.

4 Anonymous, 'An autobiography of a schizophrenic experience', *Journal of Abnormal and Social Psychology*, 51 (1955), 677–89.

5 Fuller Torrey, E., *Surviving Schizophrenia*, p. 171, © 1983 by E. Fuller Torrey. Excerpts reprinted by permission of Harper Collins Publishers.

CHAPTER 3: WHAT DO WE KNOW ABOUT SCHIZOPHRENIA?

1 Johnstone, E., Crow, T., Frith, E. and Owens, D., 'The Northwick Park "Functional" psychosis study: diagnosis and treatment response', *The Lancet*, 16 July 1988, 119–25.

2 Crow, T., 'The continuum of psychosis and its implications for the structure of the gene', *British Journal of Psychiatry*, 149 (1986), 419.

3 Warner, Richard, *Recovery from schizophrenia: Psychiatry and Political Economy* (London: Routledge, 1985).

4 Davison and Bagley in *Current Problems in Neuropsychiatry*, ed. R. N. Herrington (Ashford: Headley, 1969).

5 Parnas *et al.*, 'Perinatal complications and clinical outcome within the schizophrenic spectrum', *British Journal of Psychiatry*, 140 (1982), 416–20.

6 Stabenau and Pollin, 'Early characteristics of monozygotic twins discordant for schizophrenia', *Archives of General Psychiatry*, 17 (1967), 723–34.

7 Blakemore, Colin, *The Mind Machine* (London: BBC Books, 1988).

8 Menninger, K., 'The schizophrenic syndrome as a product of acute infectious disease', *Archives of Neurology and Psychiatry*, 20 (1928), 464–81.

9   Fuller Torrey, E., *Surviving Schizophrenia*, p. 1. © 1983 by E. Fuller
    Torrey. Excerpt reprinted by permission of Harper Collins Pub-
    lishers.

10 Results of research carried out by G. Harrison and colleagues at
    University Hospital, Nottingham, reported by Eileen Ballantyne in
    the *Guardian*, 31 October 1988.

11 Sashidharan, Sashi, 'Schizophrenia – or just black?', *Community
    Care*, 5 October 1989.

12 Crow, T., 'Type I and Type II syndromes', *British Journal of
    Psychiatry*, 137 (1980), 383–6.

13 North, Carol, MD, *Welcome, Silence* (London: Simon and Schuster,
    1988).

14 World Health Organization study in twelve different countries
    carried out over eight years commencing in 1977, reported in *The
    Times*, 3 March 1986.

15 Karlsson, J., 'Genetic basis of intellectual variation in Iceland',
    Hereditas, 195 (1981), 283–8.

16 Crow, T., The Lieber Award Acceptance Lecture, 8 September
    1989, reported in *Schizophrenia Research*, 3 (1990), 99–102, Elsevier
    Science Publishers (Biochemical Division).

17 Howe, Gwen, *Schizophrenia: A Fresh Approach*, 2nd edn (Newton
    Abbot: David and Charles, 1990).

18 Carter and Watts, 'Possible biological advantages among schizo-
    phrenic's relatives', *British Journal of Psychiatry*, 118 (1971), 453–60.

19 Hoffer, A. and Osmond, H., *How to live with schizophrenia*, 2nd edn
    (London: Johnson, 1971).

20 Miles, C. P., 'Conditions predisposing to suicide: a review', *Journal of
    Nervous and Mental Disease*, 164 (1977), 231–46.

21 Wilkinson, D. G., 'The suicide rate in schizophrenia', *British Journal
    of Psychiatry*, 140 (1982), 138–41.

22 Roy, A., 'Suicide in chronic schizophrenia', *British Journal of Psy-
    chiatry*, 141 (1982), 171–7.

23 Wallace, Marjorie, 'Coroners criticized over mental patients', *The
    Times*, 21 January 1986, quoting Dr Malcolm Weller.

24 See for example Slater, E. and Roth, M., *Clinical Psychiatry*, 3rd edn
    (London: Bailliere Tindall, 1977), p. 307.

25 David, J. M., 'Overview: maintenance therapy in psychiatry', *Ameri-
    can Journal of Psychiatry*, 132 (1975), 1237–45.

26 MIND, National Association for Mental Health, *Major Tranquillizers
    – Special Report*, 1986.

27 Johnstone, E. C. and Owens, D. G. C., 'Neurological changes in a
    population of patients with C.S. and their relationship to physical
    treatment', *Acta Psychiatrica Scandinavica*, Supp. 291, 63 (1981),
    103–10.

28 Owens, D. G. C. and Johnstone, E. C., 'Spontaneous involuntary

disorders of movement', *Archives of General Psychiatry*, 39 (1982), 452–61.

29 George, Bill, 'Schizophrenia: a personal account', *Social Work Today*, 23 February 1987.

CHAPTER 4: DENIAL

1 Fuller Torrey, E., *Surviving Schizophrenia*, p. 219. © 1983 by E. Fuller Torrey. Excerpts reprinted by permission of Harper Collins Publishers.

2 Hoffer, A. and Osmond, H., *How to Live with Schizophrenia* (London: Johnson, 1971), p. 22.

3 Johnstone, E. *et al.*, *The Northwick Park Study of First Episodes of Schizophrenia*, Part I: 'Presentation of the illness and problems relating to admission', *British Journal of Psychiatry*, 148 (1986), 115–20.

4 Weleminsky, Judy, 'Drawing it all together – a blueprint for a decent service in the community', in *Schizophrenia*, ed. Katia Gilhome Herbst (Mental Health Foundation, 1987).

5 Falloon, I. and colleagues, DHSS-sponsored Buckingham Community Project, mid-1980s.

6 Crow, T. *et al.*, *The Northwick Park Study of First Episodes of Schizophrenia*, Part II: 'A randomized controlled trial of prophylactic neuroleptic treatment', *British Journal of Psychiatry*, 148 (1986), 120–7.

7 Hemmings, Gwynneth, Director General of Schizophrenia Association of Great Britain, SAGB Newsletter, June 1980.

8 Bleuler, M., 'The long term course of schizophrenic psychoses', pp. 631–6, in *The Nature of Schizophrenia*, ed. Wynne, Cromwell and Matthysse (New York: Wiley, 1978).

9 For example, see note 1 above, p. 66, and Slater, E. and Roth, M., in *Clinical Psychiatry* (3rd edn), (London: Bailliere, Tindall, 1977), pp. 308 and 311.

10 Woodman, Tim, 'First person account: a pessimist's progress', *Schizophrenia Bulletin*, vol. 13, no. 2 (1987), 330.

11 Carstairs, G. M., Rollin, H. R. and Wing, J. K., 'Informing relatives about schizophrenia', *The Bulletin of the Royal College of Psychiatrists*, vol. 9, no. 3 (March 1985), 59–60.

12 Wing, J. K., *Schizophrenia and its Management in the Community*, p. 18, published by the National Schizophrenia Fellowship from an article in *Psychiatric Medicine* (New York, 1977). This extract reprinted by permission of the National Schizophrenia Fellowship and the author.

13 See note 12 above.

14 *Mental Hospital Closures*, p. 10, published by the National Schizophrenia Fellowship in association with SANE – Schizophrenia: A

National Emergency, and reprinted by permission of both organizations.

15   See note 3 above.

16   See Howe, Gwen, *Schizophrenia: A Fresh Approach*, 2nd edn (Newton Abbot: David and Charles, 1990), pp. 65–75, for a straightforward account of this legislation and definition of the term 'nearest relative'.

17   Mary Tyler: from a unpublished survey carried out amongst members of the National Schizophrenia Fellowship, 1986.

18   See *Provision of Community Services for Mentally Ill People and Their Carers* (1990), a survey carried out on behalf of the Department of Health into the views of members of the National Schizophrenia Fellowship on community services for the mentally ill, published by the NSF.

19   See note 16 above, p. 49.

20   Birchwood, M., Cochrane, R. and Moore, B., 'Prediction of relapse in schizophrenia: the development and implementation of an early signs monitoring system using patients and families as observers', *Psychological Medicine*, 9 (1989), 649–56.

21   Reported by Mr Patrick Thompson, MP, in House of Commons debate on Mentally Ill People, *Community Care*, 1 February 1989.

22   Kay, Adah and Legg, Charlie, *Discharged to the Community: a review of housing and support in London for people leaving psychiatric care* (February 1986), funded by the Greater London Council, published by The Housing Research Group, The City University, St John Street, London EC1 4PB.

23   Research for Essex Social Services Department carried out by Catherine McLean and reported in *Social Work Today*, 13 October 1988.

24   'Personal account: Ian's story', by a befriender and NSF member, National Schizophrenia Fellowship Newsletter, May 1988.

25   *Slipping Through the Net*, published by the National Schizophrenia Fellowship, 1989.

CHAPTER 5: SOME IDEAS AND THEORIES

1   Letter from David Pilgrim, lecturer in psychology, published in *New Statesman*, 23 September 1988.

2   Fromm-Reichmann, F., 'Notes on the development of treatment of schizophrenics by psychoanalytic psychotherapy', *Psychiatry*, 11 (1948), p. 263–73.

3   Slater, E. and Roth, M., *Clinical Psychiatry*, 3rd edn (London: Bailliere Tindall, 1977), p. 264.

4   Blakemore, Colin, *The Mind Machine* (London: BBC Books, 1988), p. 124.

5   Bateson *et al.*, 'Toward a theory of schizophrenia', *Behavioural Science*, 1 (1956), pp. 251–64.

6   Fuller Torrey, E., *Surviving Schizophrenia* (New York: Harper and Row, 1983), p. 92, quoting Lidz, T., Parker B., and Cornelison, A., 'The role of the father in the family environment of the schizophrenic patient', *American Journal of Psychiatry*, 113 (1956), 126–32.

7   Wynne and Singer, 'Thought disorder and family relations of schizophrenics: I – a research strategy, II – a classification of forms of thinking', *Archives of General Psychiatry*, 9 (1963), 191–8.

8   Hersch, S. and Leff, J., 'Parental abnormalities of verbal communication in the transmission of schizophrenia', *Psychological Medicine*, I (1971), 118–27.

9   Hersch, S. and Leff, J., 'Abnormalities in parents of schizophrenics', *Maudsley Monograph*, no. 22 (Oxford University Press, 1975).

10 Liem, J. H., 'Effects of verbal communications of parents and children: a comparison of normal and schizophrenic families', *Journal of Consulting and Clinical Psychology*, 42 (1974), 438–50.

11 Wynne, Singer and Toohey, 'Communications of the adoptive parents of schizophrenics', in *Schizophrenia*, ed. Joorstad and Ugelstad (Oslo, 1975).

12 Neale and Oltmanns, *Schizophrenia* (New York: Wiley, 1980), p. 339.

13 Henry, J., *Pathways to Madness* (New York: Vintage Books, 1973), quoted in Clare, A., *Psychiatry in Dissent* (London: Routledge and Kegan Paul, 1980).

14 Barton, Russell, *Institutional Neurosis* (Bristol: John Wright and Sons, 1959).

15 Jones, Kathleen, *Experience in Mental Health* (London: Sage Publications, 1988), p. 89.

16 Laing, R. D., *The Politics of the Family* (London: Tavistock, 1971).

17 See note 16 above.

18 Hill, D., 'Psychiatric delusions', *New Statesman*, 2 August 1988.

19 Judy Weleminsky in letter to *New Statesman*, published 9 September 1988.

20 Pilgrim, D., 'The myth of schizophrenia', OPENMIND, no. 33, Summer 1988.

21 For example, Max Birchwood and colleagues at All Saints Hospital, Birmingham, and Liz Kuipers at the Institute of Psychiatry, London.

22 Wing, J. K., 'Abandoning what?', *British Journal of Clinical Psychology*, 27 (1988), 325–8, in response to Bentall, R., Jackson, H. and Pilgrim, D., 'Abandoning the concept of schizophrenia', *British Journal of Clinical Psychology*, 27 (1988), 303–24.

23 Brown *et al.*, 'Schizophrenia and Social Care', *Maudsley Monograph*, no. 17, 1966.

24 Vaughn, C. E. and Leff, J. P., 'The influence of family and social factors on the course of psychiatric illness: a comparison of schizophrenic and depressed neurotic patients', *British Journal of Psychiatry*, 129 (1976), 125–37.

25   See Howe, Gwen, *Schizophrenia: a Fresh Approach*, 1st and 2nd edns (Newton Abbot: David and Charles, 1986 and 1990), pp. 42–3.

26   Kuipers, L. and Bebbington, P., 'Expressed emotion research in schizophrenia: theoretical and clinical implications', *Psychological Medicine*, 18 (1988), 893–909.

27   Herzog, T. Heidelberg, 'Nurses, patients and relatives; a study of family patterns on psychiatric wards', manuscript for publication in the conference proceedings, *Family Intervention in Schizophrenia*, Milan, 1 November 1988.

28   MacMillan, J. F. *et al.*, *The Northwick Park study of first episodes of schizophrenia*, Pt IV, 'Expressed emotion and relapse', *British Journal of Psychiatry*, 148 (1986), 133–43.

29   McCreadie, R. and Phillips, K., The Nithsdale Schizophrenia Survey VII: 'Does relatives' high expressed emotion predict relapse?', *British Journal of Psychiatry*, 152 (1988), 477–81.

30   For example, see Slater, E. and Roth, M., *Clinical Psychiatry*, 3rd edn (London: Bailliere Tindall, 1977), p. 261.

31   Lintner, Brenda, *Living with Schizophrenia* (London: Macdonald Optima, 1989), p. 34.

CHAPTER 6: MUDDLED THINKING

1   Quoted from the introductory booklet 'SANE' (1987), produced by SANE – Schizophrenia: A National Emergency, and quoted with that organization's permission.

2   Jones, Kathleen, *Experience in Mental Health* (London: Sage Publications, 1988), p. 92.

3   See Mental Health Act 1983, published by HMSO.

4   Birley, J., letter to National Director of National Schizophrenia Fellowship, published in *Psychiatric Bulletin*, 14 (1990), 235–6.

5   See, for example, Carol North's *Welcome, Silence* (London: Simon and Schuster, 1988).

6   Det. Supt. Tom Williamson speaking in BBC TV Byline Special programme 'Whose mind is it anyway?', 1 August 1988.

7   Treffert, D. A., 'The practical limits of patients rights', *Psychiatric Annals* 5(4) (1971), 91–6, quoted by Chodoff, Paul, in 'The case for involuntary hospitalization of the mentally ill', *American Journal of Psychiatry*, 133 (1976), 5.

8   Terry Hammond, when Manager of The Society of St James, Southampton, in a talk given at a seminar held by the Mental Health Foundation at the Royal Society of Medicine, London, on 16 December 1986, reported by Katia Gilhome Herbst in *Schizophrenia*, published by the Mental Health Foundation.

9   Wallcraft, Jan, in 'Openmind', October/November 1986.

10   Blakemore, Colin, *The Mind Machine* (London: BBC Books, 1988).

11   George, Bill, extract from article in *National Schizophrenia Fellowship*

Newsletter, May 1988, and quoted with permission of National Schizophrenia Fellowship.

12 Hoffer, A., in *Medical Applications of Clinical Nutrition*, ed. Bland, Jeffrey, PHD, (New Canaan, CT: Keats Publishing Inc. 1983).

13 Gurling, Hugh, in 'Eliot Slater Memorial Lecture', Institute of Psychiatry, 6 October 1988.

14 Dexter, G. and Wash, M., *Psychiatric Nursing Skills – a Patient-Centred Approach* (London: Croom Helm, 1986), introduced as a 'core text for psychiatric nurses in training'.

15 CCETSW paper no. 19.25, 'Refresher Training for Approved Social Workers', February 1990.

16 Roger Freeman, Health Minister with special responsibilities for the mentally ill, speaking in House of Commons, reported by Sheila Dawes in *Social Work Today*, 18 January 1990.

17 *That's Life* 'special' on Mental Illness, BBC TV, 9 April 1989.

18 Valerie Robinson, when a Committee Member of VOICES.

19 World Health Organization study in twelve different countries carried out over eight years commencing in 1977, reported in *The Times*, 3 March 1986.

20 Marjorie Wallace in her award-winning series in *The Times*, December 1985.

21 See for example Falloon, I. and Talbot, R., 'Persistent auditory hallucinations: coping mechanisms and implications for management', *Psychological Medicine*, 11 (1981), 329–39.

22 For example, Wallace, Marjorie, 'Mad, bad or simply sad' in *The Forgotten Illness* © Times Newspapers Ltd, 1987, and BBC TV Byline special programme, 'Whose mind it is anyway?', 1 January 1988.

23 Wallace, Marjorie, 'Who cares, who suffers?', Monday Page, *The Times*, 7 March 1988, © Times Newspapers Ltd.

CHAPTER 7: DOWN A SLIPPERY SLOPE

Introductory excerpt from Fuller Torrey, E., *Nowhere to Go.* © E. Fuller Torrey. Reprinted by permission of Harper Collins Publishers.

1 Reported in Fuller Torrey, E., *Nowhere to Go*, p. 159. © 1983 E. Fuller Torrey. Reprinted by permission of Harper Collins Publishers.

2 Marjorie Wallace in *The Forgotten Illness*, published by Times Newspapers Ltd, p. 13.

3 'Denying the mentally ill', editorial in *The New York Times*, 5 June 1981.

4 Baxter, E. and Hopper, K., 'Homeless in New York City', *American Journal of Orthopsychiatry*, 52 (1982), 393–408.

5 Article in *The New York Times*, 14 July 1985, reported in Fuller

Torrey, E., *Nowhere to Go* (New York: Harper and Row, 1988), p. 134.

6   Langsley, D. G. (when President of the American Psychiatric Association) and Robinowitch, C. B., 'Psychiatric manpower: an overview', *Hospital and Community Psychiatry*, 30 (1979), 749–55.

7   Fuller Torrey, E., *Surviving Schizophrenia*, p. 139. © E. Fuller Torrey 1983. Reprinted by permission of Harper Collins Publishers.

8   Edwina Currie, House of Commons Question Time, reported in *Social Work Today*, 5 May 1988.

9   Peter Walker, Secretary of State for Wales, in foreword to *Mental Illness Service Strategy For Wales*, published May 1989.

10   Jones, Kathleen, *Experience in Mental Health* (London: Sage Publications, 1988), p. 20. © K. Jones.

11   Jones, K. and Poletti, A., 'The "Italian experience" reconsidered', *British Journal of Psychiatry*, 148 (1986), 144–50.

12   Jones, K. and Poletti, A., 'The mirage of a reform', *New Society*, 4 October 1984.

13   See note 10 above, p. 67.

14   Edwina Currie, quoted in article by David Fletcher, Health Services Correspondent, *Daily Telegraph*, 29 November 1988.

15   House of Commons Social Services Committee's Second Report: *Community Care* (London: HMSO, 1985), para. 162.

16   Wallace, Marjorie, 'Through an open door to despair', *The Forgotten Illness*, Times Newspapers Ltd, 1987, quoting Dr Malcolm Weller, p. 5.

17   Crisis at Christmas, reported in *Social Work Today*, 2 February 1989.

18   Malcolm Weller and colleagues, from a survey referred to in National Schizophrenia Fellowship Newsletter, August 1988, interviewing homeless people attending the Crisis at Christmas shelters.

19   See article quoted in note 14 above.

20   Lister, John, Health Panel report for Association of Local Authorities, 'London's National Health Service: forty years on', quoted in *Social Work Today*, August 1988.

21   Audit Commission, 'Making a reality of community care' (London: HMSO, 1986).

22   Mitchison, Amanda, 'Adrift in Hastings', *Independent Magazine* Issue 27 (11 March 1989).

23   National Health Service Health Advisory Service and DHSS Inspectorate report on mental health care in Hastings quoted in note 22 above.

24   COID, J., 'Rejected or accepted by the National Health Service', *British Medical Journal*, vol. 296 (25 June 1988).

25   See note 24 above.

26   J. Coid, in a talk quoted in the NSF's Oxford Group report on the National Schizophrenia Fellowship's Oxford Conference on Foren-

sic Psychiatry and the Mentally Ill Offender, 1988, reprinted by permission of National Schizophrenia Fellowship.

27 J. Coid, answering from the floor at Conference, see note 26 above.

28 Fuller Torrey, E., *Nowhere To Go* (New York: Harper and Row, 1988), p. 18.

29 Weller, M., 'Aspects of violence', *The Lancet*, 2 (1987), 615–17.

30 Taylor, P., 'The risk of violence in psychosis', *Integrative Psychiatry*, 4 (1986), 12–24.

31 Sinclair, Lydia, 'Death in a prison hospital raises serious questions', *Social Work Today*, 24 August 1987.

32 See note 31 above.

33 See note 28 above, pp. 31–2. Reprinted by permission of Harper Collins Publishers.

34 BBC TV Byline Special, 'Whose mind is it anyway?', with Marjorie Wallace, 1 August 1988.

35 Anthony Clare in a letter published in *The Times*, 6 January 1986.

36 Granada TV programme, *World in Action*, 20 November 1989.

37 BBC TV Byline Special, as in note 34 above, and Marjorie Wallace in the *Sunday Times* magazine, 24 July 1988.

38 See note 10 above, p. 160.

CHAPTER 8: BACK TO MEDICINE

1 Hill, David, 'Psychiatric delusions', *New Statesman*, 12 August 1988 (discussed in Chapter 5 of this book).

2 World Health Organization, *Schizophrenia: an International Follow-up Study* (New York: Wiley, 1979).

3 Kety, S., 'From rationalization to reason', *American Journal of Psychiatry*, vol. 131, no. 9 (September 1974), 961.

4 Kallman, F. J., *The Genetics of Schizophrenia* (Locust Valley, NY: J. J. Augustin, 1938).

5 Kallman, F. J., 'The genetic theory of schizophrenia: an analysis of 691 Schizophrenia Twin Index Families', *American Journal of Psychiatry*, 103 (1946) 309–22.

6 Slater, E., *Psychotic and Neurotic Illnesses in Twins* (London: HMSO, 1953).

7 Heston, L., 'Psychiatric disorders in foster home reared children of schizophrenic mothers', *British Journal of Medicine*, 112 (1966), 819–25.

8 Rosenthal *et al.*, 'The adopted away offspring of schizophrenics', *American Journal of Psychiatry*, 128 (1971), 307–11.

9 Kety, Rosenthal, Wender and Schulsinger, 'The types and prevalence of mental illness in the biological and adoptive families of adopted schizophrenics', in *The Transmission of Schizophrenia* (Oxford: Pergamon Press, 1975).

10 Clare, Anthony, *Psychiatry in Dissent* (London and New York: Routledge, 1980), p. 183.

11 Hugh Gurling and colleagues, Middlesex Hospital, London, July 1988.

12 Colin Blakemore, *The Mind Machine* (London: BBC Books, 1988), p. 126.

13 Stabenau and Pollin, 'Early characteristics of monozygotic twins discordant for schizophrenia', *Archives of General Psychiatry*, 17 (1967), 723–34.

14 Pollin, W., 'The pathogenesis of schizophrenia', *Archives of General Psychiatry* 27 (1972), 29–37.

15 Woerner *et al.*, 'Pregnancy and birth complications in psychiatric patients: a comparison of schizophrenics and personality disorder patients with their siblings', *Acta Psychiatrica*, 17 (1973), 723–34.

16 Mednick, S. A. *et al.*, 'Breakdown in individuals at high risk for schizophrenia: possible predispositional perinatal factors', *Mental Hygiene*, 54 (1981), 50–63.

17 Owen, F. *et al.*, 'Increased dopamine receptor sensitivity in schizophrenia', *The Lancet* 2 (1978), 223–6, and Wong, D. *et al.* 'Positron emission tomography reveals elevated D2 dopamine receptors in drug-naive schizophrenics', *Science*, 234 (1986), 1558–63.

18 Owens, D. *et al.*, 'Lateral ventricular size in schizophrenia: relationship to the disease process and its clinical manifestations', *Psychological Medicine*, 15 (1985), 27–41.

19 Reveley, A., 'Cerebral ventricular enlargement in nongenetic schizophrenia: a controlled twin study', *British Journal of Psychiatry*, 144 (1982), 89–93.

20 Reveley, A., 'Cerebral ventricular size in twins discordant for schizophrenia', *The Lancet*, 1 (1984), 540–1.

21 Kennard, C. and colleagues, London Hospital, investigating rapid eye movement, etc., reported in the *Daily Telegraph*, 31 October 1988, by Malcolm Brown.

22 Lintner, Brenda, *Living with Schizophrenia* (London: Macdonald Optima, 1989), p. 68.

23 Hare, E., Price, J. and Slater, E., 'Mental disorders and season of birth', *British Journal of Psychiatry*, 124 (1975), 81–6.

24 Dalan, P., 'Month of birth and schizophrenia', *Acta Psychiatrica Scandinavica*, Supp. 203 (1968), 48–54.

25 Fuller Torrey, E., *Schizophrenia and Civilization* (New York: Jason Aronson, 1980).

26 Tyrrell, D., *et al.*, 'Possible virus in schizophrenia and some neurological disorders', *The Lancet*, 1 (1979), 839, and Crow, T. *et al.*, 'Characteristics of patients with schizophrenia or neurological disorder and virus-like agent in cerebrospinal fluid', *The Lancet*, 1 (1979), 842.

27 Fuller Torrey, E., *Surviving Schizophrenia*, p. 90. © 1983, E. Fuller Torrey. Reprinted by permission of Harper Collins Publishers.

28 Colin Blakemore, *The Mind Machine* (London: BBC Books, 1988), p. 126.

29 Slater, E. and Roth, M., *Clinical Psychiatry*, 3rd edn (London: Bailliere Tindall, 1977), p. 307.

30 World Health Organization study in twelve different countries, carried out over eight years, reported by Marjorie Wallace in *The Times*, 3 March 1986.

31 Bender, L., 'Childhood schizophrenia', *Psychiatric Quarterly*, 27 (1953), 3–81.

32 Graff, H. and Handford, A., 'Coeleac syndrome in the case histories of five schizophrenics', *Psychiatric Quarterly*, 35 (1965), 306–13.

33 Dohan, F., Grasberger, J. and Lowell, F., 'Relapsed schizophrenics: more rapid improvement on a milk- and cereal-free diet', *British Journal of Psychiatry*, 115 (1969), 595–6.

34 Singh, M. and Kay, S., 'Wheat gluten as a pathogenic factor in schizophrenia', *Science*, 191 (1976), 401–2.

35 Hemmings, W., 'The entry into the brain of large molecules derived from dietary protein', *Proceedings of the Royal Society* (London), 200B (1978), 175–92.

36 Zioudrou, C., Streaty, R. and Klee, W., 'Opioid peptides derived from food proteins; the exorphins', *Journal of Biological Chemistry*, 254 (1979), 2446–9.

37 Dohan, F., 'Schizophrenia and neuroactive peptides from food', *The Lancet*, 1 (1979), 1031.

38 Wood, N. *et al.*, 'Abnormal intestinal permeability – an aetiological factor in chronic psychiatric disorders?', *British Journal of Psychiatry*, 150 (1987), 853–6.

39 King, D. S., 'Statistical power of the controlled research on wheat gluten and schizophrenia', *Biological Psychiatry*, 20 (1985), 785–7.

40 Gwen Howe, *Schizophrenia: A Fresh Approach*, 2nd edn, (Newton Abbot: David and Charles, 1990), Chapter 11.

41 Kinney and Jackson, 'Environmental factors in schizophrenia', in *The Nature of Schizophrenia*, ed. Wynne, L., Cromwell, R. and Mattheusse, S. (New York: Wiley, 1978), pp. 38–51.

42 Bentall, R., Jackson, H. and Pilgrim, D., 'Abandoning the concept of schizophrenia: some implications of validity arguments for psychological research into psychotic phenomena', *British Journal of Clinical Psychology*, 27 (1988), 303–24.

43 Slater, E. and Roth, M., *Clinical Psychiatry*, 3rd edn (London: Bailliere Tindall, 1977), p. 308.

44 Kety, S., 'From rationalization to reason', *American Journal of Psychiatry* (September 1974), 962.

45 See note 43 above, p. 223.

46 Johnstone, E. C. *et al.*, *The Northwick Park study of first episodes of schizophrenia*, Part I, *British Journal of Psychiatry*, 148 (1986), 115–20.

47 The Acheson Report for the DHSS on Primary Health Care in Inner London, 1981.

48 Edwina Currie, when Junior Minister of Health with special responsibilities for the mentally ill, speaking at the 1988 MIND annual conference, reported in *Social Work Today*, 8 December 1988.

49 Mary Tyler; from an unpublished survey carried out among members of the National Schizophrenia Fellowship, 1986.

50 See note 43 above.

51 Norris, V., 'Mental illness in London', *Maudsley Monograph*, no. 6 (London: Chapman Hall, 1959).

52 Sandifer, M. G. *et al.*, *Journal of Nervous Mental Disorder*, 139 (1964), 350.

53 Kendall, R. E., 'Schizophrenia: the remedy for diagnostic confusion', *British Journal of Hospital Medicine* (October 1972), 383–90.

54 World Health Organization, *International Pilot Study of Schizophrenia* (1972).

55 American Psychiatric Association, *Diagnostic and Statistical Manual of Mental Disorders*, 3rd edn (Washington, DC, 1980).

56 Stromgen, E., 'Changes in the incidence of schizophrenia?', *British Journal of Psychiatry*, 150 (1987), 1–7.

57 See, for example, Der, G., Gupta, S. and Murray, R., 'Is schizophrenia disappearing?', *The Lancet*, vol. 335 (3 March 1990), pp. 513–15, which has provoked ongoing controversy and debate.

58 Johnstone, E., Crow, T., Frith, D. and Owens, D., 'The Northwick Park "functional" psychosis study: diagnosis and treatment response', *The Lancet* (16 July 1988), pp. 119–25.

59 Richard Jameson, 'Delusions', the *Observer*, 1 July 1984.

60 Curry, S., Marshall, J., Davis, J. and Janowsky, D., 'Chlorpromazine plasma levels and effects', *Archives of General Psychiatry*, 22 (1970), 289–96.

61 See note 27 above, pp. 114–15.

62 World Schizophrenia Fellowship, *Manual on Schizophrenia: a Guide for Families*, to be published by the World Health Organization.

CHAPTER 9: ANOTHER WAY FORWARD

1 John Pringle, 'A case of schizophrenia', article in *The Times*, 9 May 1970.

2 Roger Freeman, when Minister of Health with special responsibility for the mentally ill, House of Commons adjournment debate, reported by Sheila Dawes in *Social Work Today*, 18 January 1990.

3 Gillian Shephard, MP for Norfolk, South West, quoted in report on the proceedings of House of Commons debate: *Community Care*, 1 February 1989.

4   For detailed discussion, see Howe, Gwen, *Schizophrenia: A Fresh Approach*, 2nd edn, (Newton Abbot: David and Charles, 1990), Chapters 10 and 11.

5   Leff, Julian, *Psychiatric Diagnosis: Notes for Relatives and Friends* (National Schizophrenia Fellowship, 1989).

6   Recovered sufferer and member of VOICES.

7   Valerie Robinson, when a member of VOICES committee.

8   See note 4 above, pp. 90–3.

9   Falloon, I. and Talbot, R., 'Achieving the goals of day treatment', *Journal of Nervous and Mental Disease*, vol. 170, no. 5 (1981), 279–85.

10 Wing, J. K., 'Schizophrenia and its management in the community', published by the National Schizophrenia Fellowship from an article published in *Psychiatric Medicine* (New York 1977), reprinted with permission of National Schizophrenia Fellowship and the author.

11 Ferris, J. and Wilson, F., 'Schizophrenia: opening the door', *Social Work Today*, 27 October 1988, p. 27.

12 Huws, D., speaking on BBC TV Byline Special, 'Whose Mind Is It Anyway?', 1 August 1990.

13 Newton, Jennifer, *Preventing Mental Illness* (London and New York: Routledge, 1988), p. 108.

14 Jones, K., *After Hospital: a study of long-term psychiatric patients in York* (University of York/York Health Authority, 1985).

15 See note 7 above.

16 Robyn Gardner, when a committee member of VOICES.

17 Smith, Naomi, *New Prospects for Schizophrenia* (Kera Press, 27 Altenburg Avenue, London W13 9RN, 1987).

CHAPTER 10: GETTING IT RIGHT

1   Renee Short, MP, Chair, Social Services Select Committee of the House of Commons, referring to part of the work of this Committee at a seminar held at the Royal Society of Medicine, London on 16 December 1986 and reported in *Schizophrenia*, ed. Katia Gilhome Herbst, Policy Development Officer, Mental Health Foundation, 1987.

2   Reported in *The Forgotten Illness* (Times Newspapers Ltd, 1987).

3   Letter to *The Times* from Robin M. Murray, Dean of the Institute of Psychiatry, 3 December 1988.

4   Reported in the introductory leaflet *SANE* (1987), produced by SANE – Schizophrenia: A National Emergency.

5   See note 4 above.

6   Jones, Kathleen, *Experience in Mental Health* (London: Sage Publications, 1988), p. 97.

7   See Mental Health Act 1983, HMSO publication.

8   For example, the National Schizophrenia Fellowship's dialogue with,

and written representations to, Health Ministers with special responsibility for the mentally ill, during the winter and spring of 1990.

9   Dr Trevor Turner, consultant psychiatrist at St Bartholomew's and Hackney Hospital, Director of the Community Psychiatry Research Unit, Hackney, reported by Mary Manning in *Social Work Today*, 27 October 1988.

10 *Charter of Rights*, 1990, available from the National Schizophrenia Fellowship (see Useful Addresses).

11 Chris Heginbotham, 'Little progress against discrimination', *Social Work Today*, 26 January 1989.

12 Smith, Naomi, *New Prospects for Schizophrenia* (Kera Press, 27 Altenburg Avenue, London W13 9RN, 1989).

13 See letter printed in the National Schizophrenia Fellowship Newsletter May 1987, reprinted with permission of the National Schizophrenia Fellowship.

14 Social Security Advisory Committee's report on benefits for disabled people, available from HMSO, and quoted in *Social Work Today*, 8 December 1988.

15 *Carers' Needs – a 10 Point Plan for Carers'* available from Book Sales Department, King's Fund Centre, 126 Albert Street, London NW1 7NF.

16 Gillian Shephard, MP, House of Commons Debate on Community Care.

17 Griffiths Report, *Community Care: agenda for action* (London: HMSO, 1988).

18 ICM survey sponsored by SANE and the National Schizophrenia Fellowship and published in the *Guardian*, 23 July 1990.

19 Letter to a Society of Friends working group, published in its report, *Dream or Nightmare: the closure of longstay mental hospitals and community care* (Quaker Social Responsibility and Education, Friends House, Euston Road, London NW1 2BJ, 1989).

20 See note 6 above, p. 160.

Further Reading

Kingsley Amis, *Stanley and the Women* (Harmondsworth: Penguin, 1985)
A humorous novel which brilliantly illustrates the way some of the 'muddled thinking' affects one sufferer and his family.

E. Fuller Torrey, *Nowhere to Go* (New York: Harper and Row, 1988)
An apt title for this searing indictment of the plight of many of the seriously mentally ill in the United States today.

E. Fuller Torrey, MD, *Surviving Schizophrenia*, 2nd edn (New York: Harper and Row, 1988)
Probably the most comprehensive and useful coverage of this subject that is available.

Clare Greer and John Wing, *Schizophrenia at Home* (National Schizophrenia Fellowship, 1988)
A second edition of a book first published in 1974 which shows that little has changed for families trying to cope with this illness. Available from the National Schizophrenia Fellowship (see useful addresses).

Gwen Howe, *Schizophrenia: A Fresh Approach*, rev. 2nd edn (Newton Abbot: David and Charles, 1990)
Useful general introduction by the present author, which includes chapters on the mental health legislation, resources in the community and a detailed discussion on a dietary approach to schizophrenia.

Kathleen Jones, *Experience in Mental Health* (London: Sage Publications, 1988)
Compares various models of community care and discusses the problems of attempting to implement this without any prior relevant research.

Carol North, MD, *Welcome, Silence* (London: Simon and Schuster, 1988)
A vivid and informative autobiography of her own experience of a long schizophrenic illness by a practising American psychiatrist.

Marjorie Wallace, *The Forgotten Illness* (London: Times Newspapers Ltd, 1987)
A reprint of the award-winning series of articles in *The Times* during December 1985, with a selection of the correspondence that followed. Available from SANE and the National Schizophrenia Fellowship (see Useful Addresses).

Terry Hammond and Pat Wallace, *Housing for People Who Are Severely Mentally Ill* (London: National Schizophrenia Fellowship, 1991)
Available from the National Schizophrenia Fellowship (see Useful Addresses).

Useful Addresses

Please enclose a stamped addressed envelope with any correspondence.

National Schizophrenia Fellowship
28 Castle Street
Kingston-upon-Thames
Surrey KT1 1SS
Tel: 081-547 3937

Concerned with helping those affected by schizophrenia and allied disorders, with improving services and promoting education and knowledge. Regular newsletters and conferences. Local self-help groups and community projects throughout the country.

VOICES Forum
Based at NSF London Advisory Centre
197 King's Cross Road
London WC1 9BZ
Tel: 071–837 6436

Run by schizophrenia sufferers for sufferers, with regular meetings in London and local groups evolving in various parts of the UK.

CONCERN
c/o Dr Malcolm Weller
52 Friern Barnet Road
London N11 3BT

For health professionals and laypeople concerned with the plight of the homeless mentally ill.

Schizophrenia Association of Great Britain
International Schizophrenia Centre
Bryn Hyfryd
The Cresent
Bangor
Gwynedd, LL57 2AG
Tel: 0248 354048

Actively involved in research to find a biochemical cause and cure for this illness. Provides a newsletter and updates on exciting work sponsored by the Association at Bangor University.

Making Space (formerly the North West Fellowship)
46 Allen Street
Warrington
Cheshire WA2 7JB
Tel: 0925 571680

Concerned with assisting sufferers and families in the North of England and promoting community care facilities, education and research.

SANE (Schizophrenia: a National Emergency)
6th Floor
120 Regent Street
London W1A 5FE
Tel: 071–434 0150

Raises funds for research and, on a smaller scale, for community projects. Campaigns to raise awareness of the problems caused by schizophrenia and for better care for sufferers and relatives.

MIND (National Association for Mental Health)
22 Harley Street
London W1N 2ED

Concerned with mental handicap and mental health issues. Local groups, affiliated to MIND, organize drop-in centres, group homes and other facilities.

Disability Alliance
25 Denmark Street
London WC2H 8NJ

Publishes the best and most comprehensive handbook on benefits and allowances for the disabled, updated annually.

Manic Depression Fellowship
13 Rosslyn Road
Twickenham
Middlesex TW1 2AB

A lively and expanding organization which produces an interesting newsletter four times a year.

Index